A Flavor of
Provence

A Flavor of
Provence

Katy Holder and Susie Ward

Illustrations by Paul Collicutt

CHARTWELL
BOOKS, INC.

A QUARTO BOOK

Published by Chartwell Books
A Division of Book Sales, Inc.
114 Northfield Avenue
Edison, New Jersey 08837

This edition produced for sale
in the U.S.A., its territories
and dependencies only.

ISBN 0-7858-0581-8

This book was designed and produced by
Quarto Inc.
The Old Brewery
6 Blundell Street
London N7 9BH

SENIOR EDITOR Kate Kirby
DESIGNER Suzie Hooper
SENIOR ART EDITORS Anne Fisher, Liz Brown
TEXT EDITOR Deborah Savage
PICTURE RESEARCHER Susannah Jayes
ILLUSTRATOR Paul Collicutt
PICTURE RESEARCH MANAGER Giulia Hetherington
EDITORIAL DIRECTOR Mark Dartford
ART DIRECTOR Moira Clinch

Typeset in Great Britain by Central Southern Typesetters, Eastbourne
Manufactured in Hong Kong by Regent Publishing Services Ltd
Printed in China by Leefung-Asco Printers Ltd

Contents

The translucent blue-green depths of a calanque. Such warm-water fjords punctuate the coast between Marseilles and Cassis, and are accessible only by foot or boat.

Historical, administrative and travelers' Provence all vary somewhat in their delineations, and writers draw their boundaries accordingly. Structuring our epicurean portrait using the modern departments, we have taken in the eastern reaches of the Gard along the Rhône, the Bouches-du-Rhône, the Vaucluse, the Var, and the southern halves of the Alpes Maritimes and the Alpes de Haute-Provence. It thus includes hill, tableland, and river valley Provence, and the Côte d'Azur.

For all its modern surface sophistication and the tourist hordes that crowd its beaches and magazine-feature towns and villages, Provence remains an elemental place. It is the sun and wind that rule.

Introduction

marshes of the Camargue and scattered lagoons boil ominously, and all vegetation wilts under the constant buffeting; then, as suddenly as it arrived, the sandy haze lifts, the sky clears and all is as blue as the famous shutters on Provençal windows.

There are other colors which are typically Provençal, derived from nature and the fancies of man, rather than from tricks of the light. The hill towns are either the grey-white of Gordes and Peillon or the ochre of Roussillon and Entrevaux, seemingly growing from the crags on which they perch or based in the earth pigment so much in evidence in the paintings of Cézanne and Van Gogh. East along the coast, the colors burst into brilliant contrasts: against the unwinking blue of sea and white of sand bloom the pinks, pale oranges, greens and yellows of café awnings, umbrellas and yacht sails. Inland, hues are more muted: in the flat heartland from Aix-en-Provence to St-Rémy, it is the thirsty green of patchy grass, of plane tree *allées* and cypress windbreaks; on the Vaucluse plateau, pale mounds burst into purple glory with the seasonal blooming of lavender. Farther east, it dries to the greys of rock, olive and mountain thyme.

In the hinterland of the Riviera around Grasse thrive the raw materials of the French perfume and crystalized-flower industry – rose, jasmine, bitter-orange flowers, mimosa, violets, geranium, mignonette and, again, lavender. On the coast itself, cut flowers are a key crop. Over 8,900 acres are

VISIONS OF PROVENCE

The sun brings the wealthy retired, celebrities and attendant curious, romantic travelers and lovers of antiquities, to bask in the air of well-being and infectious opulence it imparts. It enriches the farmers and vinters, attracts artists, and casts highlights and shadows – seen nowhere else except perhaps Greece – onto the old stones and pastel plasters of the villages.

Of the 30 or more local winds identified by the region's great poet and conservator of tradition, Frederic Mistral, that with which he shares his name – the *mistral* – is the undisputed master. Originating in the north of Europe and picking up power over the Alps, it sweeps through the corridor of the Rhône into the heart of the region 10 months of the year, reaching as far east as St Raphael and as far west as Nîmes and Montpellier. It can blow so hard that the skin goes numb, the brain itself seems to wither, and those caught in its wake cannot hear themselves speak. Its reign is as unpredictable as it is temperamental. For three or four days, trees in orchards and *allées* rustle and sway, the

Ever since Van Gogh took his easel to the south, sunflowers and Provence have been linked in popular imagination. Today these bright fields inspire EU subsidies for vats of cooking oil rather than art.

devoted to outdoor plants, among them marigolds, pinks, anthemis, violets, anemones, tulips and freesias, while out-of-season glasshouse varieties include chrysanthemums, roses, carnations and gerbera. The proof of these yearly contributions to the national product delights both eye and nose.

Lastly, lost in its own world at the mouth of the Rhône, is the unique Camargue, where colors are seen as if through a photographer's filter. On warm days, its blue-green lagoons, far-stretching rice fields, dazzling white salt flats and fabled white horses appear as a shimmering mirage; at the height of the *mistral* or in the bleak days of winter, the atmosphere can turn overtly threatening and even repellent, everything bathed in a dark grey wash.

THE LIVING PROVINCE

Most of these visions of Provence are as true today as they were three-quarters of a century ago, when the "gilded youth" and self-exiled writers of the United States turned the Côte d'Azur from a winter to a summer playground, and the *garrigue* – or scrubland – of the hills and plateaux was

home to *Jean de Florette* and *Manon des Sources* of Marcel Pagnol's combined memory and imagination. What has changed is the overall prosperity of the region and the numbers who enjoy it.

Today, its cities and large towns draw visitors from all over France – and sometimes the world – to their well publicized festivals. In the month before Christmas, Marseilles hosts its enormous Santons Fair, devoted to traditional clay or wooden crib figurines in the garb of Provençal peasants and tradesmen; in the three weeks before Shrove Tuesday, flower-strewn revelry breaks out at Nice's Mardi Gras; in summer, Orange gives its great Roman theatre over to opera and concerts; the churches and public halls of Aix-en-Provence thrill to the strains of its Music Festival and the doyenne of party-givers, Avignon, revels in all things antic: everything from the Palace of the Popes to the humble street-corner is commandeered by drama troops, mime artists, singers, dancers, magicians and medieval pageants.

Smaller towns and villages capitalize on their history and associated customs. Stes-Maries-de-la-Mer – on a spit of land at the mouth of the Rhône but seemingly at end of the earth – attracts thousands of gypsies and spectators for three days every May. Its Pilgrimage to the Shrine of St Sara celebrates their adopted patroness, the legendary black servant of the three Holy Marys, who left Israel by sail-less boat after the death of Christ. Mary Magdelene, one of the three Marys, has her own festival and pilgrimages at Châteaurenard and at St-Baume; while St Martha, another passenger in the boat, is commemorated – along with the *tarasque*, the marauding dragon whom she vanquished – at the annual fête in Tarascon. The monster, now a figure of fun, parades through the streets snapping and swishing its tail at the screaming, giggling crowds that line the route.

INFLUENCES MYSTIC AND MYTHIC

Though most fêtes and festivals ostensibly celebrate Christian legend, their roots tap deep into earlier memories of Greek and Roman Provence. Sometimes they reach even deeper, to a time when Celtic tribes inhabited scattered *oppida* (fortified towns), whose remains can be found near modern centres like Aix-en-Provence and Nîmes, as well as in rural situations such as the Luberon hills and the desolate Crau plain, east of the Camargue. The many pilgrimage sites dedicated to the Virgin or local saints have often displaced less inhibited deities – earth mothers and fertility goddesses who once held power over productivity of land and people.

Devotion to nature and its cycles is perhaps best expressed by what might be called a historical cult of springs or *sources*. The great Pont-du-Gard, that Roman feat, breathtaking in both its engineering and beauty, was constructed to bring the spring water of Uzes to Nîmes – the latter town itself named for the water sprite who guarded its central fountain. Only 18 miles to the southwest, the world's most publicized mineral water, Perrier, has its birth. Petrarch gave immortality to the Fontaine de Vaucluse ("the spring of the enclosed valley") which, in turn, gave its name to the department. Long before the fourteenth-century poet found tranquillity living by its usually limpid green water, the Romans had written of the "impetuous torrent" that transforms this deepest (at present thought to be 1,010 feet) of the world's springs into one of the most powerful (rising from 15 feet per second to 328 feet per second at full flow). Today, though the path to its basin is

Gordes, in the Vaucluse region (or Peillon in the Comtat de Nice). Villages Perchés ("perched villages") are a characteristically charming counterpoint to the flatlands of the Bouches-du-Rhône and the coastal strip.

like that to a secular Lourdes, packed end to end with tourist memorabilia and nougat stands, its impressiveness has not diminished. In contrast, the glorious fountains which give Aix its special character are but a remnant of the 60 springs which made the town a thermal resort in antiquity. But in the human scale, the spring about which Pagnol wrote in his two affecting novels is probably the most important. For its literary existence merely confirms the truth that water was, indeed, the very *source* of life to all who lived in this deceptively lovely, sometimes capriciously harsh, environment. A drought can still wreak havoc in this part of the world.

As the Roman's favored first province (hence the name Provence), the region benefited from imperial investment, both monetary and technical. Whereas the original Greek colonists had been traders, founding the great port of Marseilles and forging a route up the lower Rhône, the Romans were not only consummate urban planners – with Arles, Nîmes, Orange and Aix as living monuments – but innovative agriculturalists. By channeling springs and introducing new species to the barren hills, what we now so romantically imagine as the typically Provençal landscape was created. As their legacy, the Romans left the olive, fig, lemon, cypress and plane tree and the vine. The first and the last of these are the basis of major industries which flourish there today.

The Olive – Symbol of Provence

The production of olive oil is indeed a commercial pursuit nowadays, though quality oils are still made by small growers and co-operatives. The terms *vierge* (virgin) – unadulterated olive juice pressed without heat – and *extra* or *fine* – an acidity rating – tell the buyer little more than the basics. But the rich, full flavors of the best oils command prices much in excess of ordinary supermarket olive oils, and reflect the judgement of the grower/millers, the variety of the olive, the climate and soil, as well as the fact that artisanal production is a dying trade. The groves have been decimated by frosts and floods in the 1980s and 1990s and independent production is at the mercy of larger corporations and modernity. Even among the artisan-makers, the old coconut mats once used for holding the olive paste have gone the way of tourist-market doormats; nylon discs do their job, while the hydraulic press has replaced the donkey and millstone.

Among the most highly regarded oils are those of the independents and the co-operative of Maussane, near St-Rémy. A deep, thickly translucent green, the color is the result of olives harvested young. In contrast, the oil of Nyons, to the northeast, is a golden bronze, because the Tanche olive from which it is made is harvested and crushed when ripe – and black. Though there are some 60 varieties of edible olive, only about 20 are exploited locally, and of these the Picholine, Tanche, Lucques and Nice are the most frequently encountered.

The Picholine is perhaps the quintessential Provençal olive. Small, green and pointed, it becomes the traditional *olive cassée* – "broken olive" – whose flesh is split by a hammer and ultimately pickled in aromatic brine flavored with herbs and orange peel. It can be found in every *traiteur* and at outdoor market stalls in every town in Provence.

In addition to the virgin oil made from the first cold pressing and the fruit itself, the olive tree has always been a generous provider for the local economy. From secondary

The fabled white horses of the Camargue graze on marsh grasses. Legend makes them descendants of Roman cavalry animals.

and later pressings come oil for cooking and soap-making. The dried pulp is then used for fertilizer and the stones ground for lubricating oil. The wood of the tree is highly prized, so those that have been felled by wind, frost or age are sculpted into statues or turned into salad bowls, mortars and pestles, serving utensils and other small items that, together with the olive oil and herb soaps, and the newer, more recherché pressed oils – *huile de pignon* (pine nuts), *noisette* (hazelnut) and *pistache* (pistachio) – sell for extravagant prices in chi-chi boutiques.

SALT AND SEASONINGS

The herbs that perfume the soaps, candles and sachets and compose the pre-packaged *herbes de Provence* may, unfortunately, have become the hackneyed fodder of tourist Provence; but if souls have a scent, the pungent smells of garlic, lavender, rosemary, small-leaved basil, sage, fennel, oregano, wild and cultivated thyme, *sarrigue* (savory) and juniper surely characterize the soul of Provence. They enliven stuffings and sauces, are used in marinades and for basting roasted meats and birds, lend distinction to traditional vegetable *tians* (casseroles), *gratins*, *sautées* and *purées*, and even appear in sorbets (tomato and basil) and ice creams (lavender and honey).

Herbs infuse the alcoholic drinks of the region – particularly *pastis*, whose idiosyncratic smell of aniseed (close cousin of fennel) permeates the nostrils of both drinker and those seated nearby. Claimed by Marseilles as its own, *pastis* has moved from being the typical Provençal

drink featured in the postcard cliché of bereted old men seated outside village-square cafés; now it's becoming the pre-prandial tipple of all red-blooded French males. Several brands fight for the market, but the distillers Pernod-Ricard dominate the commercial brands. This is heady popularity indeed for an early twentieth-century invention that began as an unwelcome substitute for the wormwood-based *absinthe* fashionable in *fin-de-siècle* France; the latter was outlawed because of the brain damage suffered by heavy imbibers. Lovers of *pastis* insist that, like all the fennel family, anis aids the digestion (they are strangely silent about more cerebral effects).

When the guidebooks and agricultural profiles refer to Provence as "the garden of France," the automatic pictures conjured up are usually those of the widely distributed *olivettes* and almond groves, of wheat and maize fields between Arles and Tarascon, of the lavender and *lavandin* (a less costly hybrid) beds of the Vaucluse and Gard departments, of the rich market gardens of the Rhône plain, and of flocks of the famously tasty sheep of the limestone moors (*garrigues*) and Crau plain. Less apt to spring to mind is the dull, flat alluvial delta of the Camargue, but that too is of growing importance.

While the wild southern Camargue was designated a botanical reserve in 1928 and a nature reserve in 1970, the northern region has been extensively drained of salt water and irrigated with fresh, producing huge tracts of arable land. Most of the produce farmed in the heartland of Provence is represented here, but in the 1960s, rice became king. Nowadays the acres devoted to its cultivation have been reduced, but the dyked waters submerging the green shoots are still a notable presence, providing 30 per cent of all rice sold in France. The introduction of "gourmet varieties" like "red" rice demonstrates the constant search for new possibilities to exploit and new markets to conquer.

But the Camargue's greatest contribution is neither animal or vegetable. It is a mineral, yet one of the most important edible products on earth: salt. Mining the salt marshes has been a local industry since Roman times, and the name of the medieval walled town Aigues Mortes ("Dead Waters") – once on the sea but now becalmed west of the brown, grey and white salt pans – testifies to the longtime barrenness of the southern Camargue. Over 27,000 acres east and west of the Petit Rhône are pumped to form a

sodium chloride solution; then the dried and crystalized salt is raked and shovelled into 65-feet high *camelles* or mountains at the rate of some 16,500 tons a day. The Compagnie Salins du Midi, which controls this highly lucrative industry, is an important presence in the region, since it also controls the largest (if not the most impressive) wine company on the coast, Listel.

WINE AND CHEESE

Wine is an expanding interest in Provence. As with salt, the development of viniculture in the region was the brainchild of the Romans and, at one time, Provençal wine was considered a worthy rival to that grown in the Ligurian hills around the imperial capital. But the fall of Rome and the decline in the local economy through succeeding centuries meant that, by the 1960s, much of Provençal wine production was of very poor quality.

A notable exception was the land between Avignon and Orange, cultivated and coddled by the Popes and anti-Popes as their private vineyard; this area successfully survived the assault of time to become the second-largest appellation contrôlée in France: Châteauneuf-du-Pâpe. Any of 13 varieties of grape – a particularly liberal number – are allowed in the individual make-up of any Appellation d'Origine Contrôlée (AOC) Châteauneuf-du-Pâpe, but the distinctive flavor of grenache is always apparent. The greater part of the production is red, though the white is excellent and over-subscribed. Other Rhône AOCs within the Provençal demarcation include some Côtes-du-Rhône, Gigondas, Vacqueyras, Sablet, Seguret and the popular sweet Beaumes-de-Venise.

Vineyard workers during the annual vendage (grape harvest) in the Côtes-de-Provence.

What most people mean when they speak of Provençal wines lies further south. This area – together with that farther west in the Languedoc-Roussillon – has seen a vinous renaissance since the unhappy days before 1960. Now government support and private investment have seen it dubbed the "California of France," a soubriquet somewhat justified by the experimental attitude of many of the new young winemakers and the imaginative substitution of new grape varieties for the sometimes tired old ones. Côtes-de-Provence is the largest Provençal appellation, mainly known for its fruity rosés, but red and white wines are improving.

Bandol (AOC) produces hearty, velvety reds, as well as delicious whites and rosés, while Cassis (AOC) delivers a respectable crisp white. Two tiny appellations – Palette, the smallest in France, with just two estates outside Aix-en-Provence, and Bellet, on the outskirts of Nice – make reds, whites and rosés that are regarded as good-value collectors' wines by those in the know.

Historically, the cheeses made to go with the local wines came from the milk of ewes and goats who could survive on the lonely *garrigues*. Among these are the *poivre d'âne* of the coast and near hinterland, small cakes of goat's cheese dusted with *sarrigue* (the same savory that forms part of the beast's diet); the *picadons* of villages near Avignon, another

goat's cheese, soft, semi-soft and piquantly aged; and *brousse*, an unpressed cottage cheese often mixed with herbs and served as a substitute for a full cheese plate. Banon, the most famous of the Provençal cheeses, was originally made from the milk of goats grazed on Mont Ventoux; the weighted and pressed curds shelved for a month to dry, before being wrapped in fresh chestnut leaves. Today even cow's cheese is marketed as "Banon," an unfortunate liberty. But the chestnut leaves are still *de rigeur*.

Lasting Impressions

The "cuisine of the sun" – as Roger Vergé, one of Provence's most famous chefs, calls it – has left an indelible mark on Western cooking, infusing it with a new appreciation of freshness, of bold combinations and undisguised vegetable flavors; it is repeating, in a gastronomic way, what happened a century ago when Van Gogh set up his easel in Arles and Cézanne came back to live in his hometown of Aix-en-Provence.

The former, with his friend, Gauguin, lost himself in the vivid colors of the southern landscape, made resonant by the pure air; when his demons sent him mad, the asylum outside St-Rémy became his refuge. Cézanne, besotted by the countryside around Aix, painted more than 100 canvases of Mont-Ste-Victoire alone. The modern traveler can literally follow his brushstrokes, finding recognizable views along every turn of the "Cézanne trail." These giants were followed by other greats – Renoir at Cagnes-sur-Mer; Matisse, Chagall, Modigliani, Dufy and Ernst at Nice, Vence and St-Paul-de-Vence; and Picasso at Vallauris.

As these Impressionists, Cubists, Fauves, Surrealists and many others found, Provence brought liberation. And as it freed the artists' palettes and spirits, so it has freed the food lover's palate and sense of excitement. The pleasures of the modern table owe much to this smiling land, and in the following pages of evocative text, photos and recipes, we attempt to share the tradition that is responsible.

I n the popular mind, Provence is synonymous with ripe,
luscious vegetables. It is not the meat or even the
seafood that we first think of, when we elaborate
the delights of the regional table. Rather it is the
almost erotic profusion of plump *marmande*
tomatoes, pungent garlic, fleshy artichokes, purple
eggplants and peppers of many hues that stirs the
imagination. In the fabled street markets of Nice, Aix-
en-Provence, Marseilles and Avignon, and in the hundreds
of smaller versions in towns
and villages throughout
Provence, pyramids of color
dazzle the eye; while the
perfume of truly ripe fruit and
vegetables – a luxury for
travelers from less temperate
zones and from more
urbanized cultures – mingles
with that from stalls selling
dried lavender and fresh herbs. That these colors and strong
flavors are largely preserved in the cooking strengthens our
fascination with this "cuisine of the sun."

Salads and Vegetables

THE GARDEN OF FRANCE
Provence is the garden of France, an important source of
produce for the entire country, as well as exports beyond.
From Cavaillon and Pertius come baby potatoes, asparagus,
artichokes, cardoons,

lettuces, fennel, zucchini and aubergines; from around
Carpentras, tomatoes, melons and truffles; from the Rhone
to St-Rémy, a bounty of soft fruits; while the caves of
Roussillon shelter a thriving mushroom industry.

Next to the ubiquitous tomato and its companion, the
eggplant, in the region's most famous – and most over-
exposed – local dish, *ratatouille* (*ratatouia* in Provençal), it is
probably the artichoke that commands the greatest respect
in the local kitchen, particularly in Nice. Called the "edible
flower of Provence," it is seen everywhere in season – from
tiny, chokeless specimens to be eaten whole and raw, or
stirred into flat omelets, or baked in a *tian*, to the mature

A view of the old port at Nice. Nowadays it is less of a working commercial harbor; its guests are yachts and pleasure boats.

globe or purple-tipped varieties, served hot *à la barigoule* or *à la Provençale*, or cold, with *aïoli* or a vinaigrette made of the finest Maussane olive oil and a tangy wine vinegar.

Marinated artichoke hearts are sometimes included in recipes for *pan bagnat*, the soggy but utterly delicious contribution of Nice to the international sandwich pantheon. Thick open-textured bread – or a special roll – is sliced and spread with olive oil, and then packed with tomatoes, peppers, onion slices and anchovy fillets, augmented with a personal selection from pitted olives, radishes, hard-boiled egg, and the said artichokes. It can be weighted and left to "ripen" for an hour or two before eating, to make it even more finger-lickin' good.

A SALAD OF RENOWN

But the most renowned contribution of that city is probably *salade Niçoise*, which has as many variations as there are chefs. The classical version had nothing cooked in it; ideally, it contained some salad leaves, topped by quartered (*not* sliced) tomatoes, black olives, green pepper, radishes, baby *fèves* (lima-type beans) when in season, and marinated anchovy fillets. The oily dressing included *pissalat*, a marinated sardine and anchovy purée. The modern additions of cold, sliced potatoes, green beans and tuna may be unorthodox, but they are welcome to most palates.

Less celebrated abroad, but beloved of the Niçoise, are their *tourtes*, thin-crusted savory pies that are appreciated as snacks or first courses and sold by *traiteurs* throughout the town. Fillings include spinach and mint; potato, pumpkin and zucchini; and Swiss chard (*blette*), a pinch of sugar, pine nuts, raisins and egg. *Troucha de blea*, the Niçoise version of *tian de blette*, combines these last ingredients with artichokes and peas; in Aix both cardoons and chard are prepared in a cream cheese sauce. A wide variety of vegetable *tians* – named for the stoneware dishes originally manufactured in Carpentras – almost always including tomatoes, and sometimes salt fish and/or egg, are popular all over Provence.

Though Marseilles is the hometown of *pissaladière*, the "Provençal pizza," it has been enthusiastically adopted by the rest of the south. In the old days, it could be found on almost every street corner of the old town, sold in heavy slices by vendors and bakeries. Today its original bread-dough base has often been adapted to a lighter puff pastry, and it has become the stock-in-trade of *traiteurs* and *pâtissières*. Despite this aberration, it should *never* have cheese; tomato sauce is a debatable point. In its purest form, the dough is covered with a thick layer of onions sautéed in olive oil, mashed and filleted anchovies, and black olives – all else is superfluous.

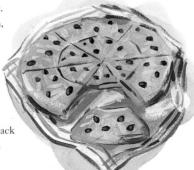

Of Provence's three famous vegetable soups, *aïgo boulido* can hardly claim the adjective, at least historically. Its name means "boiled water" and – like the "nothing" soups of other cultures – it was made with water, bones, garlic, olive oil and herbs, when the larder held no more. Stirring in chunks of day-old bread kept the wolf from the door. Now more bourgeois versions add tomatoes, grated cheese, leeks and even potatoes, while a variation, *soupe à l'ail*, generously augments the number of garlic cloves. Nice's *soupe au pistou* derives its name and distinctive flavor from the addition of *pistou* (page 76) to what is really a French *minestrone*. Like so much else, this most cosmopolitan of Mediterranean cities has managed to distill what it wants from other cultures and mark it as its own.

A quiet time at the Place aux Aires market in Grasse. Not for nothing is Provence styled "The Garden of France."

Pan Bagnat

SOAKED BREAD

Particularly wonderful on picnics on hot summer days, a pan bagnat
*is bread soaked in olive oil and then stuffed with anything remotely Provençal!
The tuna can be replaced with anchovies if preferred.*

Good bread, baked daily, is a Frenchman's patrimony.

MAKES 4 FILLED LOAVES

1 thin French stick (baguette)	2 ounces black pitted olives, roughly chopped
1 garlic clove, halved	6 ounce can of tuna, drained and flaked
6 tablespoons extra-virgin olive oil or olive oil	6 fresh basil leaves, roughly torn
3 firm, ripe tomatoes, sliced	Salt and freshly ground black pepper
1 green bell pepper, seeded and thinly sliced	
4 scallions, thinly sliced	

1 Cut the French stick in half lengthwise through the middle and remove a little of the dough to form a hollow. Rub each half with the garlic and then liberally sprinkle the olive oil over the bread.

2 Layer one half of the bread with the salad, olives and tuna. Scatter the basil leaves over and season well.

3 Place the remaining bread half on top, cut into four, and wrap all four sandwiches in foil. Leave for at least an hour, to allow the flavors to mingle and the oil to soak through the bread.

4 Preferably, serve on a sun-drenched beach!

Le Grand Aïoli

AÏOLI FEAST

*This is one of the most famous dishes of Provence. Traditionally served on a
Friday, because its main component is often salt cod, it is a feast of fish, vegetables,
snails and eggs all surrounding a large pot of* aïoli *(garlicky mayonnaise).*

SERVES 4–6

1 pound salt cod
4 chicken breasts
1 pound baby potatoes,
unpeeled
4 carrots, cut in batons
4 ounces green beans
8 small artichokes or a can
of artichoke hearts
12 snails
4 small cooked beets,
quartered

2 red bell peppers, seeded
and sliced
4 hard-boiled eggs, halved
2 quantities of *aïoli* (page 76)

FOR THE VEGETABLE STOCK:
1 celery stalk
1 carrot
1 onion
1 leek
1 garlic clove
1 bouquet garni

1 Soak the salt cod in cold water for 1–2 days beforehand,
changing the water frequently.

2 To make the stock, place all the ingredients in a large
pan with 5 cups water and bring to a boil. Simmer for
25–30 minutes and then set aside to cool. Strain into a
clean saucepan.

3 Drain and then rinse the salt cod. Place it in a
large saucepan with plenty of cold water (do not
add salt). Bring just to a boil, reduce the heat, and
simmer for 8–10 minutes, until tender.

4 Poach the chicken breasts in the vegetable stock
for about 10 minutes. Boil the baby potatoes for
about 10 minutes, or until tender. Blanch the carrots
and beans for 3 minutes in boiling water. Drain and
refresh all the vegetables under cold water, to halt the
cooking process and to keep the color in the vegetables.

5 Remove the stalk and any tough outer leaves from the
artichokes and cook in the stock for 10–15 minutes.

6 Just before serving, reheat the chicken, potatoes,
beans, carrots and artichokes or artichoke hearts in the
stock. Drain the brine from the snails, rinse and cook for
3–4 minutes in the stock.

7 Arrange the feast on a large serving platter with the
beets, peppers and eggs, and place the bowl of
aïoli in the middle.

Asperges au Gratin

GRATIN OF ASPARAGUS

Asparagus is a wonderfully flavored vegetable and is often best
served on its own with butter. In this recipe, we have added just a few more
ingredients to make this expensive vegetable stretch further!

SERVES 4

1½–2 pounds green or white
asparagus
¼ cup grated Gruyère cheese
½ cup grated Parmesan
cheese
6 basil leaves, roughly
torn (optional)

1 tablespoon olive oil
Salt and freshly ground
black pepper
½ cup fresh bread crumbs
1–2 tablespoons butter

Cook's Notes

Many other vegetables can be cooked in this way,
including fried slices of zucchini and eggplant and
thin slices of fried potatoes.

1 If using white asparagus, cut the woody end off about 2 inches from the bottom. If using green asparagus, you should only need to cut 1 inch off the bottom, but sometimes it is advisable to cook one piece to see how tough the lower stems are.

2 It is easier to cook large quantities of asparagus tied in bundles. So tie the asparagus into four bundles. If you have an asparagus steamer, stand the bundles in approximately 3 inches of salted water; otherwise take the deepest pan you have, and steam the asparagus in this. Stand the bundles upright and make a foil dome to cover the tips in place of the lid. Steam for 15 minutes.

3 Drain the asparagus and untie the bundles. Pat them dry on paper towels. Combine the Gruyère and Parmesan cheeses in a bowl, with the basil leaves.

4 Grease an ovenproof dish with the olive oil, ensuring the dish is as long as the asparagus. Place a layer of asparagus across the bottom, sprinkle with some of the cheese mixture and season. Place another layer of asparagus on top and sprinkle with more cheese and seasoning. Continue layering until all the asparagus is used up. Top with the breadcrumbs, season with freshly ground black pepper and dot with the butter.

5 Place under a hot broiler and broil for 3–4 minutes until the cheese is melted and the top is golden. Serve immediately. This dish can be served as a first course or as a vegetable accompaniment.

Artichauts à la Barigoule
ARTICHOKES STUFFED WITH MUSHROOMS AND BACON

*The tender purple artichokes commonly found in Provence are best for this dish, but
if they are not available, substitute the large Breton globe artichokes. This dish
makes a substantial first course or a light main dish for serving with other dishes.*

SERVES 4

5 tablespoons olive oil
3 shallots, finely chopped
2 garlic cloves,
finely chopped
3 bacon slices, finely
chopped
2 ounces brown button
mushrooms
⅓ cup fresh
bread crumbs

3 tablespoons finely chopped
fresh parsley
Salt and freshly ground
black pepper
8 small, purple artichokes or
4 Breton globe artichokes
4 small carrots, sliced
4 celery stalks, sliced
4 garlic cloves, thinly sliced
¼ cup white wine

1 Preheat the oven to 375°F. Heat 2 tablespoons of the
olive oil in a saucepan and gently sauté the shallots and
garlic for 3–4 minutes over medium heat. Add the bacon
and sauté for another 2 minutes. Add the mushrooms and
sauté for 2 minutes more.

2 Remove from the heat and stir in the bread crumbs,
parsley and seasoning.

3 Prepare the artichokes. Cut off all but 1 inch from the
stalk, remove and discard any tough outside leaves, and
trim the tips of the leaves. Cut each artichoke in half,
scooping out any hairy choke.

4 Grease an ovenproof dish large enough to hold the
artichokes in a single layer. Arrange the slices of carrots,
celery and garlic across the bottom of the dish, sprinkle
over the remaining olive oil, and then arrange the
artichokes on top, cut-side up. Pour over the wine and
place small spoonfuls of the stuffing on each artichoke.

Cover the dish with foil and bake in the oven for 45
minutes to 1 hour. Remove the foil to allow some of the
liquid to evaporate 15 minutes before the end of cooking.

5 Serve each artichoke with some of the vegetables and
liquid. *Aïoli* may be served alongside.

Artichokes, endive and cauliflower tempt customers.

21

Tourte aux Blettes

SWISS-CHARD PIE

This is a Christmas-Eve treat, on which there are many variations throughout France. If Swiss chard is not available, spinach is a suitable alternative. It can be served as a main course or a dessert.

SERVES 4–6

2 ounces raisins	2 ounces pine nuts
2 tablespoons brandy or rum	2 eggs, beaten
1 pound Swiss chard or	⅓ cup grated mild cheese
8 ounces spinach	such as Gouda
8 ounces apples, peeled,	Grated zest of 1 lemon
cored and sliced	10–12 ounces puff pastry

1 Preheat the oven to 400°F. Place the raisins in a small bowl, add the rum and leave to soak for 30 minutes.

2 Remove the ribs from the chard leaves, or the stalks from the spinach and blanch for 2–3 minutes, until the leaves have wilted. Drain well and chop. Place the chard or spinach in a bowl and add the raisins and soaking liquid, apples, pine nuts, eggs, cheese and lemon zest. Mix well.

3 Divide the pastry in two, one piece slightly larger than the other. Roll the larger piece to fit the base and sides of an 8 inch pie dish. Grease the dish and line it with the pastry. Spoon in the filling, smoothing over the top. Roll out the second piece of pastry to fit the top. Dampen the edges of the pastry with water and lay the lid on top. Seal all around the edges and then make a pattern all around the edge, using the prongs of a fork. Cut two or three slits in the top, to allow steam to escape. Bake in the oven for 40 minutes.

4 The pie can be served hot, warm or cold and is best served straight from the pie dish.

Neighborhood street markets are found throughout Nice.

Ratatouille

PROVENÇAL VEGETABLE STEW

Ratatouille must be one of the most well known of all Provençal dishes, and many arguments rage about its true ingredients. The only rule which everyone seems to agree on is that the vegetables must be cooked in olive oil alone – no water.

SERVES 4

2 medium eggplants, cut in ½ inch slices, slices quartered
2 medium zucchini, cut in ½ inch slices, slices quartered
3 tablespoons olive oil
1 large onion, thinly sliced
1 medium red bell pepper, seeded and cut in thin strips
1 garlic clove, finely chopped
2 large tomatoes, peeled and roughly chopped
½ teaspoon coriander seeds or ground coriander
Salt and freshly ground black pepper
3 fresh basil leaves, roughly torn

1 Sprinkle the eggplant and zucchini slices with salt, place them in a colander and weigh them down with a plate. Set aside to drain for 30 minutes to 1 hour. Rinse in cold water and pat dry.

2 Heat the oil in a large saucepan and sauté the onions until soft, but not browned. Add the eggplant, zucchini, pepper and garlic, cover the pan, and cook gently for 20–25 minutes.

3 Add the tomatoes, coriander and seasoning, and cook for a further 20 minutes, until the vegetables are soft but not mushy.

4 Stir in the basil, adjust the seasoning and serve. Ratatouille can be served hot as a main dish or as an accompaniment. It can also be served cold as an hors-d'oeuvre.

Salade Niçoise

This rustic, country salad which is found in every home and restaurant
in Provence, should be prepared with only the freshest, most flavorsome ingredients.
It makes a wonderful addition to any summer picnic or meal.

Pleasure boats have overtaken Nice's tuna and sardine fleet.

Cook's Notes

Discussions between the Provençaux on the correct ingredients and presentation of a salade Niçoise can become heated! Follow these three simple rules, and then sit back with a glass of chilled white wine and eat, don't discuss! Firstly, never slice the ingredients, simply quarter them or cut them into chunks. Secondly, always serve the vegetables raw, never cooked. Thirdly, never mix anchovy fillets and tuna: use one or the other.

SERVES 4–6

4 tablespoons olive oil
2 teaspoons freshly squeezed lemon juice
1 garlic clove, quartered
Freshly ground black pepper
2 ounces anchovy fillets or an 8 ounce can of tuna in oil, drained
4 large, ripe tomatoes, quartered or cut into 8
Bunch of scallions, sliced
2 eggs, hard-boiled and sliced
½ cucumber, peeled and cut into 1 inch pieces, then quartered
1 green bell pepper, seeded and finely chopped
8 ounces young lima beans, podded and peeled, or a 14 ounce can of flageolet beans, drained and rinsed
20 black olives
4 fresh basil leaves, roughly torn

1 First prepare the dressing, to allow the garlic flavor to develop. Combine the olive oil and lemon juice, add the garlic and pepper.

2 If using anchovy fillets, cut them into small pieces. If using tuna, shred it with a fork.

3 In a large serving bowl, combine the fish with the remaining ingredients, finishing with a scattering of olives and basil leaves. At the last minute, remove the garlic from the dressing and pour the dressing over the salad.

Pissaladière

ONION AND ANCHOVY TART

This tart is a specialty of Nice and its name is derived from pissalat, *which is strongly flavored fish purée. As this is extremely difficult to obtain, anchovies can be used instead. If you prefer, use half the number of olives and cut them in half.*

SERVES 4

FOR THE DOUGH	FOR THE TOPPING
1½ cups strong white flour	6 tablespoons olive oil
1 teaspoon dried yeast	1 pound onions, sliced
1 egg, beaten	2 tablespoons finely chopped
1 teaspoon sugar	fresh herbs, such as thyme,
1 teaspoon salt	basil and rosemary
	10 anchovy fillets
	20 black olives, pitted
	Freshly ground black pepper

1 Preheat the oven to 375°F. To make the dough, sift the flour into a bowl, make a well in the center and add the yeast. Pour 3 tablespoons of warm water over the yeast and leave for 5 minutes.

2 Add the egg, sugar and salt and mix with the yeast, gradually drawing in the flour. Form into a soft dough, turn out onto a floured surface, and knead for about 5 minutes, until smooth and elastic. Transfer to an oiled bowl and allow to rise for an hour in a warm place (average room temperature will suffice).

3 Meanwhile, prepare the topping. Heat the olive oil in a saucepan and add the onions and herbs. Stir the onions to insure they are evenly coated with oil. Cover with a lid, reduce the heat and cook for 20–25 minutes, until the onions are soft. Do not allow them to brown.

4 When the dough has risen, knead it again for 1–2 minutes. Roll out into a circle about 10–12 inches in diameter. Place on a greased baking sheet.

5 Drain the anchovy fillets and cut each one in two lengthwise, to produce 20 thin fillets. Cover the top of the dough with the onions and herbs. Arrange the anchovies on the top in a lattice pattern and dot each space with an olive. Season with freshly ground pepper.

6 Leave for 5–10 minutes more, to allow the dough to rise again. Bake in the center of the oven for 25–30 minutes, until brown. Serve hot, warm or at room temperature, cut into wedges.

Soupe au Pistou

VEGETABLE SOUP WITH PISTOU

Any combination of vegetables can be used in this soup, and in Provence the combination varies with the season. In summer, it includes zucchini and leeks; in the winter, it uses more dried beans and squash.

SERVES 4

4 ounces dried white beans or a can of haricot or flageolet beans
2 carrots, sliced
1 leek, sliced
3 small zucchini, cut into large cubes
4 ounces green beans, cut into 3

Salt and freshly ground black pepper
1 pound tomatoes, peeled and chopped, or a can of chopped tomatoes
2 ounces macaroni or spaghetti, broken up
Pistou, to serve (page 76)

1 If using dried beans, soak them in water overnight. Then drain them, place them in a saucepan of clean water, and bring to a boil. Simmer for an hour. Drain and discard the liquid.

2 Place the carrots, leek, zucchini and green beans in a large saucepan and add water to cover. Season. Bring to a boil and simmer for 30 minutes. Add the tomatoes, beans and pasta and continue to simmer for a further 15 minutes. At the end of cooking, the soup should be quite thick; if too much of the liquid has evaporated, add a little boiling water to the saucepan.

3 Stir in the *pistou* and seasoning and serve immediately. Do not reheat or boil the soup after adding the *pistou*, as the cheese will become tough.

4 Alternatively you can serve the *pistou* separately and allow your guests to help themselves to cheese at the table.

The entrance to the vegetarian equivalent of Aladdin's cave.

Tian de Courgettes et Tomates

BAKED ZUCCHINI AND TOMATOES WITH PARMESAN CHEESE

*This is another very popular dish in Provence and its name comes
from the earthenware dish in which it is cooked,* le tian. *In order to reproduce
the correct consistency, an earthenware dish is a must.*

SERVES 4

3 tablespoons olive oil
1 pound zucchini, sliced
1 large onion, sliced
1 tablespoon finely chopped
fresh thyme
Salt and freshly ground
black pepper
3 large, ripe tomatoes,
roughly chopped
1 garlic clove, crushed

2 tablespoons finely chopped
fresh parsley
4 fresh basil leaves,
roughly torn
4 tablespoons freshly grated
Parmesan cheese

1 Preheat the oven to 400°F. Heat 2 tablespoons of the olive oil in a large saucepan and gently sauté the zucchini, with the onion, thyme and seasoning. Reduce the heat and cook gently for a further 20 minutes, stirring occasionally. Once cooked transfer to an earthenware dish and sprinkle over the roughly chopped tomatoes.

2 Meanwhile, combine the garlic, parsley and basil and scatter over the vegetables, along with the remaining olive oil.

3 Top with the grated cheese and bake for 20 minutes, until golden. Serve immediately, from the dish.

In Provence, the country people like their chickens scratching in the gravel outside the kitchen door. The farmer's wife knows the secret places for eggs – haybales in the barn, hidden corners in outhouse buildings, the upholstery stuffing of the clapped-out Citroën in the yard. Recent EC rulings have prevented her from selling them, unless she runs a registered and rigorously inspected business. So she restricts her supplies to neighbors, to whom she gives the eggs without charge, but with, perhaps, an understood barter system in operation – my eggs for one of your rabbits, or perhaps a punnet of dawn-picked mushrooms in season.

These eggs taste differently from supermarket eggs; their yolks are bright orange. They make marvelous mayonnaise, *aïoli* and, hard-boiled, can stand on their own as an appetizer with olive oil and lemon juice, or with the typical Provençal accents of salted anchovy fillets or tuna.

Omelets too make the most of these full-flavored eggs. The Côte d'Azur hill towns of Vence and St Paul de Vence offer *baveuse*, a runny omelet of ham or cheese. From the region around Avignon comes *crespeou*, a series of omelet layers each made with a different vegetable – eggplant, fennel, sorrel, tomatoes – whatever is in the house. It is cut and served like a cake. When young *fèves* (baby lima beans) are in season, cooks in Nice incorporate them into omelets spiked with summer savory.

A variety of fried, scrambled and poached eggs *à la Provençale* are on menus throughout the region; most feature eggplant and tomato sautéed in olive oil, sometimes with garlic. Cold jellied eggs *à la Provençale* are served in tomato halves, accompanied by potato salad, eggplant salad and *aïoli*. Antibes gives its name to a preparation composed of layered scrambled eggs and sautéed zucchini, bathed in fresh tomato *concasse*, topped with cheese, and gratinated under a broiler, as well as to eggs poached on a bed of just-hatched fish and roe. In Nice, these same hatchlings are dubbed *poutina et nouat*, and served in omelets or in deep-fried egg fritters.

Pastas and Omelets

PASTAS

Nice is the traditional capital of Provençal pastas, but nowadays elegant restaurants and *traiteurs* in nearby Cannes and other resorts are also making their own. In addition to plain ribbon pastas, ravioli (*raiolles* in *patois*) and cannelloni are filled with fennel and artichoke, spinach and ricotta, crab and spiny lobster, zucchini and bone marrow, and ever more inventive but resolutely Provençal combinations. Gnocchi, another specialty, are always made with *both* flour and potato, in the Roman style. But the typical sauce is unswervingly Niçoise – a rich and deeply-colored wine, anchovy, garlic and tarragon mixture, as earthy and deeply satisfying as life in that great Mediterranean city.

Gnocchi

POTATO DUMPLINGS

Provençal gnocchi are little dumplings made of flour and potatoes. They
can be served on their own with a little melted butter and cheese, or with a variety
of sauces. Why not try these gnocchi with the tomato sauce on page 73?

SERVES 4

FOR THE GNOCCHI DOUGH
1 pound large potatoes
1 large egg, beaten
2 tablespoons butter
⅓ cup freshly grated
Parmesan cheese
Salt and freshly ground
black pepper

About a good ¾ cup
all-purpose flour

TO SERVE
4 tablespoons butter, melted
3 tablespoons freshly grated
Parmesan cheese

Potatoes from the garden of Jean de Florette!

1 Preheat the oven to 425°F. Prick the skins of the potatoes, place them on a baking sheet and bake for an hour. Reduce the heat to 400°F.

2 Cut the potatoes in half, remove the flesh, and mash. Add the egg, butter and cheese to the mash. Season with salt and pepper. Mix in sufficient flour to form a firm mixture that does not stick to your fingers.

3 On a floured work surface, take a quarter of the dough and roll it out into a rope approximately ¾ inch in diameter. Cut the dough into ¾-inch pieces. Dip a fork in flour and flatten each piece with the back of the fork, working in a curve to give a shell pattern. Transfer the gnocchi to a floured board and repeat with the remaining dough, making about 50 gnocchi. Keep the prepared gnocchi in a single layer, rather than piling them on top of one another.

4 Bring a large pan of salted water to a boil and drop the gnocchi in a few at a time, insuring they do not touch. Reduce the heat and cook until they float to the surface, about 3–5 minutes. If they are cooked for too long they will fall apart. As soon as they float to the surface, remove them with a slotted spoon and drain on paper towels. Cook the remaining gnocchi.

5 Grease a large ovenproof dish and arrange the gnocchi in the dish. Pour over the melted butter, sprinkle over the grated cheese, and bake in the oven for 8–10 minutes, until golden brown. Serve immediately.

Crespeou

LAYERED OMELET CAKE

*Almost any vegetable can be used in this recipe, making it a good dish
for using up leftovers. However, you can also concoct some wonderful creations
with a little careful planning of the vegetables to be used.*

SERVES 4

12 eggs
Salt and freshly ground
black pepper
3–4 tablespoons olive oil
1 small eggplant, thinly
sliced, slices halved
1 medium zucchini,
thinly sliced
4–5 ounces asparagus, cut
into 1 inch pieces
20 black olives, pitted

and chopped
2 garlic cloves, finely
chopped
Handful of basil leaves,
roughly torn
Small bunch of fresh thyme,
roughly chopped
2 tablespoons butter, divided
into eight

1 Preheat the oven to 375°F. Line a baking sheet with foil and grease it.

2 In four separate bowls beat together three eggs and season. Set aside.

3 Fry the eggplant and zucchini slices in batches in the olive oil and add them to one of the bowls. Blanch the asparagus pieces in boiling water for 2 minutes, drain them and add them to a second bowl. Add the olives and garlic to the third and the basil and thyme to the fourth.

4 Melt a piece of the butter in an omelet pan or skillet over high heat and add half the contents of one of the bowls. Cook over high heat for one minute; it will still be runny. Transfer to the lined baking sheet. Continue to cook the remaining seven omelets in this way, stacking them on top of one another in a colorful pattern as they are cooked.

5 When cooking the last omelet, flip it over in the pan and then place it cooked-side up on top of the stack. Bake in the oven for 15 minutes. Remove from the oven and allow to stand for 15 minutes. Serve warm or cold, cut in slices, with a tossed green salad.

Ravioli à la Niçoise

RAVIOLI WITH MEAT AND SPINACH

The ravioli of Nice are generally smaller than those found in neighboring Italy.
Ravioli is a great way of using up leftovers, both of meat and vegetable; ravioli à la
Niçoise *is a way to use up meat left over from* boeuf en daube *(see page 60).*

SERVES 4

FOR THE PASTA DOUGH
15 ounces strong white
or all-purpose flour, plus
extra for dusting
4 eggs
Pinch of salt

FOR THE FILLING
8 ounces spinach
1 onion, finely chopped
1 garlic clove, finely chopped
6 ounces ground beef
or leftover *boeuf
en daube*, minced

1 tablespoon olive oil
1 egg, beaten
¼ cup freshly grated
Parmesan cheese
Salt and freshly ground
black pepper

TO SERVE
½ quantity *sauce tomate*
(page 73)
Grated Parmesan cheese

1 To make the dough, sift the flour into a large bowl and make a well in the center. Add the eggs, salt and 3 tablespoons of water and, using your fingertips, gradually draw the flour into the center and mix to form a soft dough. Turn out onto a floured work surface and knead for 10–15 minutes, using the heel of both hands. Form the dough into a ball and very lightly dust it with flour all over. Place the dough in a plastic bag or wrap it in plastic wrap and leave it for at least 30 minutes and up to 3 hours.

2 While the pasta rests, make the filling. Place the spinach in a large saucepan with 1 inch of water. Cook for 4–5 minutes, until wilted. Drain and chop.

3 In a large bowl, combine the onion, garlic and beef. Heat the oil in a saucepan and add the meat mixture. Cook over medium heat for 10 minutes if using pre-cooked beef, and for 20 minutes if using raw beef, stirring often. Off the heat, add the chopped spinach, egg and cheese, and season well.

4 Knead the pasta for a further 5 minutes. Divide it into eight balls and roll out one as thinly as possible on a floured work surface. Straighten all four edges with a knife. Place small amounts of the filling at 1½-inch intervals. Using a thin brush, moisten around the edges and between each filling with cold water. Roll out a second piece of dough and place it on top. Using your fingers or the handle of a wooden spoon, seal around the edges of each ravioli. Using a pastry cutter or a knife, carefully cut the ravioli into squares and dust with flour. Repeat this process with the remaining dough to make about 80 ravioli.

5 Bring a large pan of water to a boil, add the ravioli and a tablespoon of salt. Cover, bring back to a boil, remove the lid and cook for a further 8–10 minutes. Drain the ravioli in a large colander and transfer them to a warmed serving dish. Gently reheat the tomato sauce and pour it over the ravioli, mixing well. Sprinkle with cheese and pepper.

Omelette aux Artichauts

ARTICHOKE OMELET

This delicious omelet can be eaten hot, warm or cold, although it is generally eaten cold in Provence. It makes an unusual addition to a picnic; simply wrap the whole omelet in foil and cut it in wedges for serving.

SERVES 4

4 small globe artichokes	Salt and freshly ground
1 tablespoon olive oil	black pepper
6 eggs, beaten	

1 Cut the tips off the leaves of the artichokes and remove any tough outside leaves. Cut each artichoke into quarters, removing the hairy choke, if it has developed.

2 Heat the olive oil in a skillet and gently sauté each artichoke until tender, 4–5 minutes.

3 Season the eggs with salt and pepper and then pour them over the artichoke quarters. Shake the pan around, to insure the base of the pan is covered with egg mixture. Cook gently, to allow the omelet to set and the base to turn golden brown.

4 If the omelet does not set on top, place it, in the pan, under a pre-heated broiler for 2–3 minutes.

5 If eating hot, serve immediately with a crisp salad. If the omelet is for taking on a picnic, allow it to cool completely before wrapping it in foil.

Artichokes and potatoes – two good partners to aïoli.

Cook's Notes

Artichoke fields are ubiquitous in Provence and the artichoke is one of the most characteristic vegetables of the region. The different varieties include large green ones, and tiny dark brown ones, with very little, but nonetheless delicious, edible pulp. Young artichokes are often so tender that they are eaten raw in salads, or poached in white wine and garlic and eaten whole. Another particularly characteristic Provençal recipe is artichauts à la barigoule (see page 21), in which artichokes are stuffed with mushrooms, ham and garlic.

Cannelloni Farcis au Poisson et aux Epinards

CANNELLONI WITH FISH AND SPINACH STUFFING

Another typically Italian dish also found in Provence is cannelloni. The fish used
can be varied, but avoid particularly oily fish.

SERVES 4

16 cannelloni tubes

FOR THE FILLING
1¼–1½ pound Dover sole
fillets
1¼ cups white wine
2 tablespoons butter
5 tablespoons flour
1¼ cups milk
Salt and freshly ground
black pepper

1 pound spinach, tough stalks
removed

FOR THE TOMATO SAUCE
2 tablespoons olive oil
1 large onion, roughly
chopped
14 ounce can of chopped
tomatoes
1 bay leaf
Fresh thyme sprig

1 Preheat the oven to 375°F. Carefully remove any remaining bone from the sole fillets.

2 Pour the wine into a large saucepan and add the sole fillets. Cover the pan with wax paper and replace the lid. Gently simmer the fish for 5–6 minutes.

3 Meanwhile, make the white sauce. Melt the butter in a small saucepan, add the flour and cook gently for 1 minute. Pour in the milk, a little at a time, stirring constantly to remove any lumps. Season with salt and pepper.

4 Wash the spinach in plenty of cold water. Cook it in a large saucepan with no added water for 2–3 minutes, until the leaves have wilted. Drain, squeeze out any liquid, and roughly chop it.

5 Remove the fish from the poaching liquid and flake it. Strain and reserve the poaching liquid. Combine the fish with the spinach and white sauce and season. Use a small spoon to stuff each cannelloni tube with the mixture.

6 To make the tomato sauce, heat the oil in a medium saucepan, add the onion and sauté for 3–4 minutes, until it is soft. Add the remaining ingredients, including the strained poaching liquid, and cook for 5–10 minutes, with the lid on. The sauce needs to be runny, because plenty of liquid is needed to tenderize the cannelloni.

7 Grease a large ovenproof dish and lay the cannelloni side by side in the dish in a single layer. Pour over the tomato and wine sauce and bake for 45 minutes, or until the cannelloni are tender.

Omelette de Fèves à la Sarriette et Salade Mesclun

OMELET WITH LIMA BEANS AND SAVORY, WITH A MIXED-LEAF SALAD

Tiny, tender lima beans are delicious when added to this omelet and served with salade mesclun *and garlic vinaigrette.*

SERVES 4

1 tablespoon butter
8 eggs, beaten
Salt and freshly ground
  black pepper
1 pound fresh small
  lima beans, pods and
  skins removed, or
  8 ounces frozen
  lima beans, thawed,
  skins removed
2 tablespoons finely
  chopped fresh savory

FOR THE SALADE MESCLUN
7 ounces mixed salad leaves
  and herbs such as frisée,
  arugula, oak-leaf lettuce,
  chervil and tiny lettuce
  leaves

FOR THE GARLIC
VINAIGRETTE
5 tablespoons extra-virgin
  olive oil
2 tablespoons white-wine
  vinegar
2 garlic cloves, finely chopped
Salt and freshly ground
  black pepper

1 Melt the butter in a skillet over a high heat. Season the beaten eggs and pour them into the pan. Allow the bottom of the omelet to set.

2 Sprinkle the lima beans and the savory over it and allow the top of the omelet to set. The lima beans should be peeled as their skins are tough and spoil the delicate flavor of the dish.

3 An alternative way to set the top of the omelet is to place the omelet in the pan, under a pre-heated hot broiler, and broil it for 2–3 minutes.

4 Combine the vinaigrette ingredients and mix well. Serve the omelet cut in wedges, accompanied by the *salade mesclun* and the garlic vinaigrette.

Cook's Notes

This omelet can be eaten hot or cold and is suitable for taking on a picnic. Allow the omelet to cool and then wrap the whole omelet in foil and slice it on arrival. Take the salad leaves in a separate container and the dressing in a screw-topped jar. Toss the salad in the dressing on arrival.

Free-range eggs are one of the pleasures of country life.

A ny book – or any chapter in a book – on Provençal seafood must begin with bouillabaisse. At least with the name of the region's most famous seafood dish, since after that, it is every gourmet for him- or herself. No one can agree what constitutes a true bouillabaisse, any more than they can agree on how to serve it.

Most afficionados will concede that its capital is Marseilles, though that does not mean that the best examples are necessarily found in those environs: there are pretenders to the throne scattered among the restaurants of the Riviera. But it was certainly the chefs of Marseilles who evolved the basic tenets of the recipe, who claimed the result as their own, and who today have formed a "Charter Bouillabaisse," to protect the reputation of their renowned creation.

It is difficult, if not impossible, to make true *bouillabaisse* anywhere but in the south of France. The single fish without whose presence it cannot be given the title – the *rascasse* or scorpion fish – is hard to track down elsewhere. Several other fish should join it in the pot, although these can vary in number and combination. Candidates include the *chapon* (a large cousin of the *racasse*), conger eel, *rouget* (red mullet) or *grondin*

Fish and Seafood

(a relative), and *St Pierre* (John Dory); some of these are more easily available. Then there are the rockfish – small denizens of the *calanques* (fiords) around Cassis and Marseilles – who are as unremarkable as they are local, except for the almost imperceptible but unmistakable flavor they impart to the broth. The concoction must *never* include molluscs – mussels or clams – although some epicureans splurge on *langouste* (spiny lobster), which sends the price sky high.

Even if all these requirements could be met in full – like *pastis*, which comes in a bottle and therefore should taste the same wherever it is poured – something is missing without the mixture of sun, sea, smells and sounds that spells coastal Provence. However the determined home cook can produce a delectable, even if not wholly authentic,

As in Pagnol's classic book and film, Marius, fishwives still offer their twitching, silvery wares in the old port of Marseilles. The surroundings, however, are much changed.

facsimile; purists deserve to be confounded!

But there are still pitfalls to come. The name is a clue to the cooking: it means "boil," and the dish should be boiled, and quickly: no more than 15 minutes once the fish begin to be added, with the most delicate dropped in last. The broth should contain onions, tomatoes, parsley, saffron, a swirl of olive oil and a good sliver of orange peel – but does it include wine? Before serving, the larger fish are removed to a separate platter and either brought to the table whole to be filleted there, or cut into serving pieces in the kitchen. The broth is strained and decanted into a large soup tureen. Some gourmets say that the fish and the broth should be served at the same time, with large pieces of the fish dropped into soup bowls to be savoured with the broth; others call this heresy and divide the two into first and second courses.

While restaurants usually serve grated cheese and toasted croûtons, with the requisite accompaniment of *rouille* (pepper and garlic sauce), those who honour the old ways say no to cheese and insist that toast is anathema. Plain bread (or the special baker's rolls made for *bouillabaisse*) should be torn into pieces and dropped into the bowl before the soup is ladled over. *Rouille* can either be spread on the bread beforehand, or stirred directly into the soup.

Such is the palaver associated with true *bouillabaisse*. Think carefully before attempting it – as you can appreciate, the honor of Provence is at stake!

The glorious Pont du Gard was built to carry drinking water to the citizens of Roman Nîmes. Rivers like the Gard were once rich in fish and freshwater crayfish, but pollution has taken a heavy toll.

BOURRIDE

By comparison, the other great fish soup of the region, *bourride*, is relatively straightforward. There are even

die-hards who maintain that *bourride* is the better dish, a pleasure to be enjoyed without the jealous constraints that can spoil its more famous cousin. Claimed by both Toulon, Provence's great naval base, and Sète, further west along the Languedoc coast, it is also a white-fish stew but, classically, it contains no saffron and never any crustaceans. The fillets are removed from the broth and placed in bowls, together with boiled potatoes topped with fried bread. *Aïoli* is stirred into the strained broth before ladling it over everything. Simplicity itself (though some garlic hounds also spread the fried bread with *rouille*).

In the waters around Marseilles, the old-fashioned *barqueroles* (open wooden boats) bring in sardines, mackerel, anchovies, eels and small white rockfish netted close to shore. Rockfish, mentioned earlier, are the sole ingredients of one of the less prestigious, but more familiar, specialities of the region – the red, rich slightly grainy *bisque*, whose

imitators, bottled in glass jars, can be found in upscale fish markets and on supermarket shelves. This should be served with the same accoutrements – cheese, croûtons and *rouille* – as restaurant *bouillabaisse*.

THE PRIDES OF PROVENCE

Special coastal molluscs which find favor include *clovisses* (small clams), *oursins* (sea urchins) and *violets* (sea quirts). These last – coarse, rubbery and gnarled – when cut in half, expose ivory meat whose strong iodine flavor is an acquired taste. Mussels were once eaten raw, but the sad state of the Mediterranean makes that less of an attraction. Instead, they are grilled over pine needles on the beach, stuffed with herbed bread crumbs and baked, or cooked *à la Provençale*. Freshwater fish from the region can sometimes be found, but crayfish, once one of the prides of Provence, are today imported from the Baltic. The western coast of France

In the streets around the Marseilles fish market, shops such as this offer prepared bouillabaisse, prawns, langoustines and spiny lobsters boiled in court bouillon, and other delights from the deep.

As if frozen by a spell, this salmon hangs forever in mid-leap outside a poissonier in Moustiers-Ste-Marie, a village famous for its faïence pottery.

accounts for more fish sold in Provençal markets than market traders want to admit.

The *rouget* (red mullet) is the queen of Provençal fishes, a relatively new sovereign found in a roll-call of recipes, such as *terrine de rouget* (layered with artichokes and tomato), *rougets à la Niçoise* (tomatoes, garlic, anchovies and lemon juice), *à la romarin* (barbecued with rosemary), and those examples given in the following pages. Members of the court include the unlovely *racasse*, *loup* (sea perch), *daurade* (bream), *thon* (tuna), *St Pierre* (John Dory) and *lisette* (baby mackerel), which can be found at restaurants and markets inland and along the coast, from Avignon to Nice. Other, more *recherché*, dishes – Nice's *soupions* (baby squid) and *sartadagnano* (a cake of small fish hatchlings, mashed with olive oil and fried on a griddle), or Toulon's *oursinado* (fish stew thickened with sea urchins) – are today more the stuff of reminiscence than experience.

Finally, it is ironic that, even along the coast, a dish based on preserved fish should find such favor. If *rouget* is the queen, then salt cod, in the form of *brandade de morue*, is the king. Originally a specialty of Nîmes, today it is enjoyed everywhere in the province – and beyond. Its "feast day" is Good Friday (*Vendredi Saint*), though nowadays it features as the *plat de jour* on Fridays at *traiteurs* all over the country. A purée of salt cod, garlic and olive oil (with the controversial addition of milk or cream), it certainly dates from medieval times and probably before, since cod is a cold-water fish and the trick of salting was probably imparted by the much-traveled Norsemen. Be that as it may, the dish that Francois I and Nostradamus praised has changed little, and the quality of this smooth oleaginous purée is thought to be the test of a true Provençal housewife.

Moules Farcies à la Mireille

STUFFED MUSSELS

Mussels served on the half shell make a sophisticated
appetizer. This recipe is simply bursting with flavor.
Mireille *is a traditional Provençal surname.*

SERVES 4

50 large live mussels, cleaned
(see page 49)

FOR THE STUFFING
6 tablespoons olive oil
8 shallots, finely chopped
5 garlic cloves, finely
chopped

4 tablespoons finely chopped
fresh parsley
Handful of fresh basil leaves,
roughly torn
1 cup fresh bread crumbs
⅔ cup white wine
Salt and freshly ground
black pepper

1 Place the mussels in a large saucepan over a high heat, and cook, shaking the pan often. Remove the mussels as they open and discard any that do not open.

2 Heat 2 tablespoons of the oil in a medium saucepan and sauté the shallots and garlic until soft but not browned. Remove from the heat and add all the remaining stuffing ingredients, except the olive oil. Mix together well.

3 When the mussels are cool enough to handle, remove and discard one half of the shell. Preheat the broiler to hot.

4 Place the mussels in a shallow ovenproof dish large enough to hold them in a single layer. Place some of the stuffing in each mussel and sprinkle over the remaining olive oil.

5 Cook under the hot broiler for 2–3 minutes, until bubbling.

When it comes to mussels (rather than muscles), big is not always better!

Morue en Raïto

SALT COD IN AN OLD-FASHIONED SAUCE

En raïto is one of the oldest Provençal sauces and here is found accompanying salt cod. Salt cod is commonly found in Spanish and West Indian grocers. This is, traditionally, a Christmas dish.

SERVES 4

1 pound salt cod or
fresh cod
2 tablespoons olive oil
1 onion, finely chopped
3 garlic cloves,
finely chopped
1 small fennel bulb,
roughly chopped
1½ pound fresh tomatoes,
peeled and roughly chopped

⅔ cup white wine
Vegetable oil
2 tablespoons capers,
drained and rinsed
5 pickles, halved lengthwise
1 ounce black
olives, pitted
Freshly ground
black pepper

1 Soak the cod for two days in cold water, changing the water frequently. It is important to soak salted cod for a sufficient amount of time to rid it of most of the salt. Once soaked, thoroughly rinse the fish in plenty of cold water and pat it dry. Carefully remove the skin and any large bones and cut the fish into cubes approximately 1½ inches square.

2 Heat the olive oil in a large saucepan. Add the onion, garlic and fennel and sauté them for 5 minutes, until the onions are soft but not browned. Add the tomatoes and wine and leave to simmer for 10 minutes, with the lid on.

3 Heat the vegetable oil in a deep pan and deep-fry the salt cod in batches until golden brown, about 2–3 minutes.

4 Add the salt cod to the tomato sauce, with the capers, pickles and olives. Season with pepper and simmer for a further 10 minutes.

Rougets de Roche Engrillés à la Valérie

RED MULLET STUFFED WITH PROVENÇAL HERBS

*Rouget de roche (red mullet) is a small fish found in the waters of the
Mediterranean and is very common in the homes and restaurants of Provence.
This recipe is excellent for barbecuing.*

SERVES 4

8 small red mullet or 4
medium–large red mullet,
prepared as in step 1
Bunch of fresh thyme
Bunch of fresh lavender
Bunch of fresh rosemary

6 garlic cloves,
finely chopped
Salt and freshly ground
black pepper
Olive oil

1 It's best to ask the assistants at the fish counter to prepare the fish. If doing it yourself, it can be prepared in two ways. Either simply gut and scale the fish, leaving the bones in, or serve the fish gutted, scaled and with the head and bones removed. To remove the backbone, cut the head off and then open the fish out flat, skin-side uppermost. Using your thumb, push down along the backbone to loosen it. Turn the fish over and carefully pull out the backbone and all other bones. The fish is now ready to stuff. Preheat the broiler to hot.

2 Tie the herbs into 4 or 8 small mixed bunches, depending on how many fish are being used.

3 Stuff each fish with a bunch of herbs and add some garlic and seasoning.

4 Brush the outside of the fish with oil and place them under the hot broiler. Broil on each side for approximately 5 minutes, or until the fish are cooked. Alternatively, grill them on a barbecue. Serve with a crisp salad and baby potatoes or rice.

Rougets de Roche au Vin Rouge
RED MULLET WITH A RED-WINE SAUCE

This recipe calls for red mullet fillets. Get your fish market to fillet the fish and to give you the head and bones, which are needed to make a stock. You don't need much sauce, because it is strongly flavored, but double the quantity of wine if you prefer.

SERVES 4

2 tablespoons olive oil, plus extra for pan-frying
4 red mullet, filleted, bones and head reserved
3 garlic cloves, quartered
1 leek, sliced
2 shallots, roughly chopped
1 carrot, sliced
1 bay leaf
Small bunch of fresh thyme
2 tablespoons fennel seeds
1¼ cups red wine
⅔ cup vegetable stock or hot water
Salt and freshly ground black pepper

1 Heat the 2 tablespoons of oil in a large saucepan and sauté the fish heads and bones for 3 minutes. Add the garlic, vegetables, herbs and fennel seeds and cook for a further 4–5 minutes.

2 Pour in the red wine and stock or water and bring to a boil. Reduce the heat, cover and simmer gently for 25 minutes.

3 Remove the lid and continue to simmer for another 5 minutes, to allow the sauce to reduce.

4 Strain the sauce into a small saucepan and season it.

5 Heat more oil and pan-fry the red mullet fillets for 4 minutes on each side, or until cooked. Meanwhile, gently reheat the sauce. Serve the fillets with the red-wine sauce and noodles. Drink the same wine with the fish.

The fruity reds of southern Provence are ideal in this dish.

Crevettes au Pastis

PRAWNS FLAMBÉED IN PASTIS

Pastis (Pernod/Ricard) is a popular drink all over Provence and is also widely used in cooking. Here it is used to flambé the prawns, which gives them a delicate aniseed flavor. Serve them on a bed of rice or with a lightly dressed salad.

SERVES 4

6 tablespoons butter
4 tablespoons pastis
(Pernod or Ricard)
24 large prawns, peeled
and veins removed

2 teaspoons fennel seeds
Salt and freshly ground
black pepper

A trompe l'oeil painting along Marseille's Vieux Port.

1 Cut half the butter in small pieces and pour the pastis into a small jug or cup. Melt the remaining butter in a skillet and quickly sauté the prawns for 2–3 minutes. Don't cook them for longer as it will make them tough.

2 Add the fennel seeds and mix well. Pour the pastis over the prawns and quickly set light to it. Be very careful when doing this and pull your hand away quickly. Allow the flame to die out on its own or, when the flame has died down, gently blow it out.

3 Add the pieces of butter and allow them to melt. Mix well and season with a little salt and plenty of freshly ground black pepper. Serve immediately.

Cook's Notes

Pastis is a licorice-flavored drink, taken as an apéritif. The suburb of Sainte-Martine in Marseilles is the home of Ricard pastis, the most common brand in Provence. Although more usually taken as a drink, pastis appears in various recipes, from ice creams to pasta and breads.

Thon à la Provençale

TUNA WITH PROVENÇAL VEGETABLES

Tuna steaks make a substantial main meal. Here they are served
in a colorful dish, using the traditional Provençal vegetables: tomatoes,
peppers and olives. Serve simply with rice or baby potatoes.

SERVES 4

2 tablespoons olive oil	Salt and freshly ground
1 small onion, finely chopped	black pepper
2 garlic cloves, finely	2 large red bell peppers
chopped (optional)	2 large green bell peppers
2 pounds ripe tomatoes,	4 tuna steaks
peeled and roughly chopped	2 ounces black
1 teaspoon sugar	olives, pitted

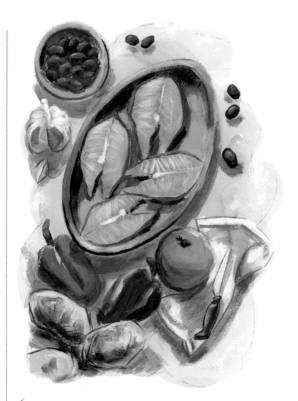

1 Heat a tablespoon of the olive oil in a saucepan, add the onion and garlic, and sauté for 3 minutes, until soft. Add the tomatoes, sugar and seasoning, and leave to simmer, covered, for 15 minutes.

2 Meanwhile, skin the peppers as follows. Place the whole peppers under a hot broiler and broil them for 10 minutes, turning them occasionally to ensure that all sides are evenly cooked. Allow the skins to char, but do not let them burn so much that the flesh inside also burns. Remove the peppers from the broiler, place them in a plastic bag, and seal the bag. Leave for 10 minutes.

3 Once the tomato sauce has cooked, remove it from the heat, allow it to cool slightly, and then press it through a strainer or purée in a blender.

4 Preheat the oven to 350°F. Remove the peppers from the bag and peel away the skins. Cut each pepper into strips approximately ½ inch wide.

5 Heat another tablespoon of oil in a skillet and pan-fry each tuna steak on both sides, for 3–4 minutes.

6 Meanwhile, grease an ovenproof dish large enough to hold the tuna steaks in a single layer. Place the steaks in the dish and cover them with the tomato sauce. Then add a layer of the peppers and top with the olives. Bake in the oven for 15 minutes.

Brandade de Morue

PURÉE OF SALT COD

Considering that so much of Provence is on the sea, it is perhaps surprising to find a recipe for salt cod that is eaten all over Provence. The addition of garlic is optional: add it during cooking or use it to rub the sides of the serving dish.

SERVES 4

1 pound salt cod
¾ cup milk
scant 1 cup olive oil
1 garlic clove (optional),
finely chopped or quartered
Pinch of ground
white pepper

TO SERVE
Olive oil
6 slices of white bread,
cut in 4 triangles each
1 garlic clove,
halved

1 Soak the cod for 1–2 days in cold water, changing the water frequently. It is very important to soak the salted cod for a sufficient amount of time, or the whole dish could be ruined!

2 Drain the fish and place it in a large saucepan of cold water. Cover the pan and bring the water to boiling point. Reduce the heat and poach the fish for 6–8 minutes, or until just tender. Drain and let the fish cool slightly. Flake it with a fork, discarding any skin and bones. If the fish is too tough to flake, pull the flesh apart with your hands and separate into small pieces.

3 Pour the milk into a saucepan and heat it gently. In a separate saucepan, gently heat half the oil. Reduce the heat to very low and add the flaked cod, beating vigorously with a wooden spoon. Stir in the finely chopped garlic, if using.

4 Keeping the cod over a low heat, add tablespoons of the hot milk and of the remaining oil alternately. Continue until all the oil is used up, and then continue to add the milk, a tablespoon at a time. If it is added too quickly the purée will become too thin. If the purée is too thick, add additional tablespoons of milk. Season with white pepper and transfer to a warmed serving dish.

5 Heat the oil in a skillet and fry the bread triangles until crisp and golden on both sides. Rub with the cut side of the garlic and serve with the *brandade*.

Moules à la Provençale

MUSSELS WITH GARLIC AND TOMATOES

Nowadays à la Provençale *indicates the presence of garlic and tomatoes in a dish.
However, a hundred years ago and earlier it simply meant "with garlic," because
tomatoes were not then an important ingredient in Provençal cooking.*

SERVES 4

2 pounds live mussels
1¼ cup white wine
2 tablespoons butter
1 onion, finely chopped
1 garlic clove, finely chopped

6 medium tomatoes, peeled
and finely chopped
3 tablespoons chopped
fresh parsley
Salt and freshly ground
black pepper

1 To clean the mussels, place them in a large bowl of water and scrape, scrub and remove the beard from each one individually, placing them in a second bowl of water when cleaned. Discard any that are broken or open. Change the water once again and leave for a further 10 minutes. Drain and run cold water over the mussels for a further 5 minutes, to insure all grit and sand is removed.

2 Place the mussels in a large saucepan over a high heat, with one glass of the wine, and cover the pan with a lid. Cook for 1–2 minutes over a high heat, shaking the pan continuously until the mussels open.

3 Transfer the mussels to a warmed serving dish, discarding any that remain closed. Pour the cooking liquid through a fine strainer.

4 Melt the butter in a saucepan, add the onion and garlic, and sauté for 2 minutes, stirring occasionally. Add the tomatoes, remaining wine and cooking liquid, bring to a boil and simmer for 5 minutes. Stir in the parsley and season the sauce. Pour it over the mussels.

Serve thick, crusty bread slices to mop up mussel sauce.

La Bourride

WHITE FISH SOUP

This recipe can be made with one type of fish only if you prefer. The aïoli *in this dish is an enriched version of a traditional* aïoli, *containing an additional two egg yolks; like* bouillabaisse, *this is often served in two stages.*

SERVES 4

3 tablespoons olive oil
1 pound leeks, finely sliced
1 fennel bulb, finely sliced
Strip of orange peel
Strip of lemon peel
Sprigs of fresh thyme
1 pound fish, such as
monkfish, bass and sea
bream, sliced thickly
⅞–1¼ cups white wine
Salt and freshly ground
black pepper

1 quantity *aïoli*
(see page 76),
made with an additional
2 egg yolks

FOR THE CROÛTONS
4 thick slices of bread, cubed
2 tablespoons olive oil

1 Heat the olive oil in a large saucepan, add the leeks and fennel, and cook gently for 5 minutes. Add the orange and lemon peels and thyme. Place the pieces of fish on top and cover with equal quantities of water and wine, ensuring all the fish is covered with liquid. Season. Bring to a boil, reduce the heat and simmer gently for 10 minutes.

2 Using a slotted spoon, remove the fish to a warmed serving dish and keep it warm. Strain the stock and add the liquid to the *aïoli*, a spoonful at a time. When the sauce becomes liquid, add the remaining stock, return to a low heat and cook gently until the sauce thickens. Do not allow the sauce to boil, because it will curdle.

3 To make the croûtons, place the cubes of bread in a bowl, sprinkle the oil over and toss well. Place the cubes on a baking sheet and bake in the oven for 10 minutes, or until golden brown.

4 Transfer the soup to a warmed bowl and serve with the croûtons. Bring the platter of fish to the table halfway through the meal, and serve with some boiled potatoes.

The catch is in at the Quai des Belges, Marseilles.

Bouillabaisse

PROVENÇAL MIXED FISH SOUP

In common with all fish soups and stews, the more kinds of fish used in a
bouillabaisse *the better; there is general agreement that you should use at least four.*
Fish such as monkfish, sea bass, bream, John Dory and snapper are all suitable.

SERVES 4-6

Large pinch of saffron
threads, mixed with 3
tablespoons hot water
6 tablespoons olive oil
3–4 garlic cloves, crushed
1 pound mixed firm
white fish fillets, cut in
2-inch pieces, trimmings
reserved
2 onions, finely chopped
2 leeks, finely chopped
2 celery stalks, sliced
Bouquet garni
8 ounces tomatoes, peeled,
seeded and chopped
Grated zest of one orange
½ teaspoon fennel seeds

Salt and freshly ground
black pepper
1 tablespoon pastis (Pernod
or Ricard)
1 tablespoon tomato paste
2 tablespoons chopped
fresh parsley

TO SERVE
1 loaf of French bread, cut
into slices
1 garlic clove, halved
1 quantity *rouille*
(see page 74)
Freshly grated Gruyère
cheese

1 Preheat the oven to 400°F. To make the *bouillabaisse*, place the saffron, 3 tablespoons of olive oil and half the garlic in a bowl. Add the fish and toss to coat. Cover and marinate for at least 30 minutes and up to 2 hours.

2 To make the fish broth, add the fish trimmings to a large saucepan with half the onions, leeks and celery, and 5 cups water. Add the bouquet garni and bring to a boil. Skim off any foam and then simmer for 30 minutes. Strain and set aside.

3 Heat the remaining olive oil in a large saucepan and sauté the remaining garlic, onions, leek and celery for about 5 minutes, stirring constantly. Add the tomatoes, orange zest and fennel seeds and cook for a further 2–3 minutes.

4 Pour in the fish broth, season and bring to a boil. Then reduce the heat and simmer gently for 10 minutes, stirring occasionally. Stir in the marinated fish, raise the heat and boil quickly for 8–10 minutes. Reduce the heat and simmer for another 5 minutes, until the fish is just cooked through.

5 Meanwhile place the slices of French bread in the oven and toast for 2 minutes. Then rub each side with garlic.

6 *Bouillabaisse* is traditionally served in two dishes: one for the fish and one for the broth. Remove the fish from the soup with a slotted spoon, transfer it to a warmed serving dish and keep it warm. Remove the bouquet garni and transfer the soup to a warmed bowl or soup tureen. Whisk the pastis and tomato paste into the broth. Sprinkle the fish and broth with chopped parsley and serve, accompanied by the *rouille* and French bread in separate dishes. To eat, place a slice of bread in the bottom of a soup bowl, sprinkle with some cheese and a dollop of *rouille*. Spoon the broth on top and eat. Follow this with pieces of fish lightly moistened with the broth.

Loup de Mer au Fenouil, Façon Yvette

SEA BASS BROILED WITH FENNEL

*Fish flavored with fennel is a very traditional French dish.
This is my friend Yvette's version. The traditional dish calls for fennel twigs,
which are hard to find; instead, Yvette uses fresh fennel.*

SERVES 4

2 tablespoons olive oil, plus extra for brushing
1 sea bass, weighing about 2–2¼ pounds, gutted and with gills removed

1 fennel bulb, sliced thinly
1 teaspoon fennel seeds
Salt and freshly ground black pepper

1 Heat the 2 tablespoons of olive oil in a large saucepan. Add the fennel and sauté for 4–5 minutes, or until soft. Stir the fennel occasionally, being careful not to break up the slices.

2 Wash and pat dry the sea bass and place the fennel seeds in the stomach cavity. Make 3–4 deep cuts on both sides of the fish.

3 Preheat the broiler to high. Line a broiling pan with foil, brush it with olive oil, and lay the slices of fennel along the foil. Place the sea bass on top of the fennel, brush it with more oil and season generously. Place the broiling pan about 4 inches away from the broiler and broil the fish on each side for 10–12 minutes, occasionally brushing the fish with oil. Turning the fish over can be quite tricky, so use a couple of fish slices or long serving implements.

4 Carefully remove the fish to a warmed serving platter and give a few slices of fennel with each serving.

Sardines en Escabèche

PRESERVED SARDINES

This is a delicious dish of cold sardines that have been spiced and preserved in vinegar. They can be eaten on the day or kept for up to five days in the refrigerator. They are perfect served as part of an antipasto.

SERVES 4

5 tablespoons olive oil
2 garlic cloves, crushed
2 onions, finely chopped
1 bay leaf
Fresh thyme sprig
Fresh rosemary sprig
2 red chilies, sliced

⅔ cup red-wine vinegar
2 pounds small,
fresh sardines
3 tablespoons all-purpose
flour, seasoned

1 Heat 2 tablespoons of the oil in a saucepan and sauté the garlic and onions over medium heat for 2–3 minutes. Add the bay leaf, herbs and chilies, and continue to cook for a further 2 minutes, or until the onions are softened but not browned. Pour in the vinegar and ⅔ cup water and simmer for 10 minutes.

2 While the sauce is simmering, wash the sardines and wipe off any scales. Pat them dry. Slit the belly and remove the stomach with a finger. Coat the fish in seasoned flour.

3 Heat the remaining oil and quickly fry the fish until golden on both sides. Place the fish side by side in a shallow dish and pour over the sauce. Allow to cool.

4 Cover the dish and refrigerate. Serve cold on its own, or as part of a selection of cold dishes.

Blue skies, still water in Cannes port and old town.

While nowadays the Provençal way with meat is heralded as health-conscious and therefore *à la mode*, such was not always the case. In much of the region before the Second World War, there was little meat to be had. In the uplands of the Var, Vaucluse and the Comtat de Nice, the butcher's shop would open only for Christmas, Easter and high saint's days. The people balanced their poverty of meat with a diet of heavy breads, salt fish and seasonal vegetables and fruit – luckily in a climate where the seasons were kind. When meat *was* available, the best cuts went to the local châteaux and the hotel trade; the peasantry made do with the off-cuts and offal.

But there were two sources that even the poor could exploit: hunting and making their own *charcuterie*. So developed the rich tradition of cured mountain hams (*jambon de montage*), pâtés of pork and game, salamis of quail, the air-dried beef (*secca*) of the Basse Alpes, and sausages of many kinds. These last, together with hillocks of green and black olives, are

A wall mosaic in a boucherie (Butcher's shop) along the Cours Saleya, a wide street branching from the coast road into Nice, marking the site of the town's pre-16th century ramparts.

Meat, Poultry and Game

still familiar accompaniments to a glass of chilled white or rosé wine under a summer arbor. And any of the above charcuterie may appear among the usual first courses in local restaurants and homes.

CELEBRATED SAUSAGE

Perhaps the most celebrated of these products is the *saucisson d'Arles*, granted its own *appellation contrôlée*.

Uniquely among French sausages, its makers do not have to declare its contents and, in the past, these have included bull, horse and donkey meat. Invented by a Bolognese butcher working in its namesake city, the *saucisson* was created to overcome a chronic shortage

An open-air meat stall in the Sunday market at L'Isle sur la Sorgue, one of the most picturesque in the Vaucluse.

of pork in nineteenth-century Provence. Today's tastes decree otherwise, and most commercial brands sold in regional towns have a large percentage of pork and some beef in them. However, among the small outfits which still make their own are those who swear that a proportion of donkey is the signature of a true *saucisson d'Arles*, providing its characteristic dry texture and acrid flavor.

A specialty also found at charcuterie counters from Orange to Aix-en-Provence are *caillettes* ("little quails") – a Provençal cross between faggot and meatloaf. A combination of chopped pig's liver, pork fat (sometimes with a proportion of minced pork), spinach and several herbs, it is wrapped in pig's caul and baked. Sold in individual *barquettes* or cut from a larger loaf, it can be reheated or served cold.

Another dish using minced meat is *sou-fassum* – the Provençal name for stuffed cabbage leaves (*chou farci*). A specialty of both Grasse and Antibes, the leaves envelope a mixture of garlic, chopped cabbage, rice, minced pork and

veal, bound with egg. The packages are gently simmered in broth. A Niçoise variation is *capoun*, in which the cabbage is replaced by Swiss chard leaves, and the stuffing is more piquant and herby.

PROVENÇAL GAME

As for game, it is scarcer now than in the days when the characters of Pagnol's *Jean de Florette* could find their dinner in the hills. Venison, quail and pheasant are mainly farmed; a few wild boar roam but most are reared behind high wire-fences. While partridge and woodcock continue to make infrequent targets, rabbit and hare bound over the scrub, there for the squeeze of the trigger. They end up in *civets* (casseroled in their blood and wine) or stewed *à la Provençale*, with garlic, tomatoes and olives.

Of domestic birds, chicken, turkey and guinea fowl boast free-range lives and, of farm animals, lamb and beef are the most characteristic of the area. Sheep roam the high places – the Luberon Mountains around Apt, the Durnace Valley

and wine, simmered in an earthenware *daubière*. In local restaurants, *daube* is sometimes offered under its Provençal title, *adola*. The meat should always be marinated for a day before cooking – most recipes specify a hearty red wine, like a Bandol; others insist on white, an unusual exception to the normal rules. Camargue cattle are perhaps the most rugged of all. Because of this, *estouffade à la Camargue* and *boeuf à la gardiane* (with added olives and named for the lone cowboys of the salt marsh) are two local beef and wine dishes which require extended cooking. The Camargue is also home to flocks of ducks, which are often partnered with olives in sauces and stuffings in Provençal kitchens.

For better cuts of beef, it is off to the Riviera for *filets au beurre d'anchois* (steak with anchovy butter) and *entrecôte à la Niçoise* – with tomatoes, baby potatoes, artichokes and olives – the same treatment given to *poulet sauté Niçoise*. Nice also prefers its own version of a legendary Vauclusean classic, *pieds et pacquets* ("feet and packages") – sheep or pork tripe, stuffed with pork, garlic and herbs, slow-cooked in tomato sauce. In Nice, they style it *tripe à la Niçoise*, but then confound the food critics by adding the trotters long missing from the original. Provençal cuisine is full of such contradictions – unlike the lavender, it is not cut and dried.

between Digne and Sisteron, and the Apilles east of Arles. Their meat is tender and sweet from the herbs that comprise their rocky pasturage; it commands good prices. Some is even awarded its own *appellation*. In Aix, a *gigot* (leg) of lamb may be roasted with lavender, in Apt basted with honey, and around Cannes rubbed with a paste of garlic and wine. Kid (*chevreau*) roasted with rosemary is a traditional alternative at Easter on the Côte d'Azur.

Provençal beef, on the other hand, usually needs long cooking, hence the evolution of *boeuf en daube* – the combination of prime braising steak, onions, carrots, herbs

This shingle, with its proud-looking young bull, hangs outside a shop in the Var – although it is a region more renowned for its succulent, herb-flavored lamb.

Poulet Rôti de Chèvre et d'Ail

ROAST CHICKEN WITH GOAT'S CHEESE AND GARLIC

*This is a simple way of roasting a chicken and giving it masses
of flavor. Goat's cheese is a common sight in the markets in Provence,
when frequently a whole cheese is preserved in olive oil and herbs.*

SERVES 4

3½–4 pound chicken
2 heads of garlic,
plus 3 cloves
2 ounces soft goat's cheese
6 fresh basil leaves,
roughly torn

Salt and freshly ground
black pepper
2–2¼ cups chicken stock
1 tablespoon butter, cut in
small pieces

1 Preheat the oven to 375°F. Wash and pat dry the chicken and reserve any giblets. Peel and halve the three extra garlic cloves and use one half to rub the skin of the chicken. Place the remaining halves in the cavity of the chicken.

2 Place the goat's cheese in a bowl and mash it. Add the torn basil leaves and seasoning. Mix well. Loosen the skin from the breast of the chicken and carefully spread the cheese mixture between the skin and flesh of the chicken. Smooth the skin back over the cheese and tie the legs together neatly.

3 Place the chicken in a roasting pan and pour the stock around it. Add any giblets. Dot the pieces of butter on the chicken and season it with salt and pepper. Put the heads of garlic in the stock.

4 Roast the chicken for about 1½ hours, basting it occasionally during cooking.

5 Remove the chicken to a warmed serving dish and keep it warm. Remove and discard the giblets. Skim any fat from the pan juices. Carefully squeeze the heads of garlic to release the soft flesh from each clove. Mash the garlic flesh into the gravy.

6 Bring the gravy to a boil over a high heat. Boil rapidly for a minute, to reduce it slightly. Season the gravy. When carving, insure each diner receives some of the goat's cheese stuffing, with the chicken and gravy.

Gardiane d'Agneau

LAMB STEW WITH BLACK AND GREEN OLIVES

This is a specialty of the Camargue region, named for the cowboys who roam the salt marshes of the area. Serve it with rice, another characteristic product of the area, cultivated on much of the Camargue's reclaimed land.

SERVES 4

2 tablespoons olive oil
8 lean lamb chops
2 onions, halved and sliced
2 garlic cloves,
finely chopped
4 tomatoes, peeled and
chopped, or 1 small can of
chopped tomatoes
4 juniper berries
Fresh rosemary sprig

Fresh thyme sprig
1 bay leaf
⅔ cup dry
white wine
1 ounce green olives, pitted
and halved
1 ounce black olives, pitted
and halved
Salt and freshly ground
black pepper

1 Heat the oil in a casserole and gently fry the lamb chops until sealed. Add the onions and garlic and cook gently for a further 4–5 minutes, until the onions are softened but not browned.

2 Add the tomatoes, juniper berries, herbs, wine and ⅔ cup water. Cover the dish, reduce the heat, and simmer for 45 minutes.

3 Add the olives and continue to cook, uncovered, for a further 15–20 minutes, or until the lamb is tender. Check the seasoning.

Some 20 types of olive are cultivated in Provence.

Bœuf en Daube

BEEF CASSEROLE

Of the score of recipes for this dish, all versions must be cooked for several hours and many also marinate overnight. The orange imparts a characteristic accent.

SERVES 4-6

2–3 pounds rump or round steak, cut into 1-inch cubes
1 onion, sliced
2 garlic cloves, finely chopped
2 carrots, sliced
1¼ cups red wine
Piece of orange peel
Sprigs of fresh thyme, rosemary and parsley and a bay leaf, tied into

a bouquet garni
Salt and freshly ground black pepper
1 tablespoon olive oil
4 ounces smoky bacon, diced
1¼ cups hot beef stock or hot water
2 ounces black olives, pitted (optional)

1 Put the meat cubes in a large bowl. Add to this half the onion slices, the garlic, carrots, wine, orange peel, bouquet garni and seasoning. Marinate overnight to allow a delicious flavor to develop.

2 Preheat the oven to 250°F. Drain the meat and vegetables, reserving the marinade liquid. Heat the oil in a casserole and sauté the bacon pieces for 2 minutes. Add the onion slices not used in the marinade, and the beef, and fry for about 5 minutes. Add the garlic and orange peel from the marinade and 2 tablespoons of the reserved marinade. Cook for 1 minute more.

3 Pour in the remaining marinade and add any remaining vegetables and the bouquet garni. Pour over the stock or water. Season.

4 Cover the pot with wax paper and a lid and cook in the very slow oven for 4–5 hours. Skim off any fat 30 minutes before the end. Add the olives (if using) and continue cooking with the lid off, to reduce the liquid slightly. Serve directly from the casserole dish.

The olive harvest is the high-point of the farming year.

Cook's Notes

Daubes can be made in advance and actually benefit from reheating. If you decide to make this in advance, it may be easier to remove the fat when it's cold.

Gigot d'Agneau Rôti d'Ail de Romarin et d'Anchois

ROAST LEG OF LAMB WITH GARLIC, ROSEMARY AND ANCHOVIES

A simple alternative to a plainly roasted leg of lamb, rich with traditional Provençal flavors: garlic, rosemary and anchovies.

SERVES 4-6

2½ pounds leg of lamb
16 small fresh rosemary sprigs
3 garlic cloves, thinly sliced
4 anchovy fillets, quartered
2 tablespoons olive oil

Salt and freshly ground black pepper
4 tablespoons white or red wine
2 tablespoons butter, cut in small pieces

1 Preheat the oven to 375°F. Place the lamb in a roasting pan and, using a small knife, make about 16 slits in the meat about 1 inch apart down the back of the lamb.

2 Into each slit, put a sprig of rosemary, a slice of garlic and a piece of anchovy. Each flavoring should be sticking out about halfway from each slit.

3 Spoon over the olive oil and season generously with salt and pepper. Roast for 25 minutes per pound, plus an additional 25 minutes. For rare meat, reduce the cooking time by 25 minutes. Baste the lamb with the meat juices a couple of times during cooking.

4 Transfer the lamb to a warmed serving dish, cover it with foil, and let it rest for 10 minutes. Skim the fat off the juices and stir in the wine. Use a wooden spoon to scrape the bits off the bottom of the pan and then stir in the butter. Check the seasoning and serve with the lamb.

Chou Farci

STUFFED CABBAGE

This version of a classic dish is from Grasse. It is difficult to make for less than 6–8 people, but a whole, stuffed cabbage makes a spectacular centerpiece at a dinner party. Serve with boiled potatoes and mustard.

SERVES 6-8

1 green cabbage
About 5 cups rich beef or
veal stock

FOR THE STUFFING
8 ounces Swiss chard or
spinach, green parts only
3½ ounces salt pork, chopped
in small pieces
2 tablespoons olive oil

2 onions, chopped
2 garlic cloves, chopped
2 large tomatoes, peeled
and chopped
4 ounces frozen peas
1 pound sausage meat
2 large eggs, beaten
Salt and freshly ground
black pepper

1 Remove any wilted or damaged outer leaves from the cabbage and trim the stalk. Wash it thoroughly under plenty of cold water. Bring a large pan of salted water to a boil and blanch the cabbage for 15 minutes. Drain and refresh it in plenty of cold water, which will help to retain its vibrant green color. Leave the cabbage upside-down in a colander until cooled.

2 Meanwhile, make the stuffing. If using Swiss chard, blanch it in boiling, salted water for 4–5 minutes. Drain and refresh it, squeezing out as much liquid as possible. Then chop. If using spinach, simply wash it and put it in a large pan with no additional water and cook for 2–3 minutes, until the leaves are wilted. Drain, squeeze out any moisture, and chop.

3 Blanch the pieces of salt pork for 2 minutes; then drain and reserve them. Heat the oil in a large saucepan and sauté the onions and garlic for 4–5 minutes, until soft but not browned. Add the chard or spinach, tomatoes, peas and sausage meat and cook for a further 4–5 minutes. Remove the stuffing from the heat and add the pork, eggs and seasoning. Mix well.

4 Gently open the cabbage leaves and remove the heart. Roughly chop this and add it to the stuffing. Mix well.

5 Starting at the center of the cabbage, replace the heart with four or five spoonfuls of stuffing mixture. Then insert layers of stuffing between the leaves. If there is any stuffing left over, increase the amount in the middle.

6 Carefully gather the leaves together, using the stuffing to hold the cabbage in shape. Traditionally, the dish would now be wrapped in a net, specifically for making *chou farci*. If you wish you can wrap the whole cabbage in a clean dishtowel to imitate this procedure. However, the cabbage will also cook perfectly well if placed core-end down in a saucepan into which it fits quite snugly. Pour the stock all around and bring to a boil. Reduce the heat, cover, and let it simmer for 2½ hours.

7 Carefully remove the cabbage with two slotted spoons and transfer it to a warmed serving dish. Bring the cabbage to the table in one piece, surrounded by a little of the cooking stock. Cut the cabbage into thick slices, with some of the stock as an accompaniment. Serve the remaining stock separately. Any leftover stock makes a wonderful base for a soup for the next day.

Lapin à l'Ail

RABBIT WITH GARLIC

This is a quick and simple dish which is full of flavor. If you prefer, chicken can be used instead of rabbit, with similarly mouth-watering results. Twenty garlic cloves may sound like a lot, but their strong flavor is reduced during cooking.

SERVES 4

3 tablespoons olive oil
1 rabbit, cut into 8 pieces, or
4 skinless, boneless chicken
breasts, halved
20 garlic cloves, bruised
1¼ cups white wine
2 teaspoons corn-starch

3 tablespoons chopped
fresh parsley
3–5 tablespoons heavy cream
(optional)
Salt and freshly ground
black pepper

1 Heat the oil in a large casserole and seal the rabbit or chicken pieces on all sides, for about 5 minutes.

2 Add the garlic and white wine. Cover and bring to a boil. Simmer for 30 minutes, or until the meat is cooked.

3 Remove the meat to a warmed serving dish. Using a potato masher or wooden spoon, carefully mash the garlic cloves, which should be fairly soft, into the cooking liquid.

4 Mix the corn-starch with a little warm water and add it to the casserole. Increase the heat under the casserole and boil rapidly to reduce the liquid. Add the chopped parsley and cream (if using) and heat through. Check the seasoning, adjusting as necessary.

5 Pour the sauce over the rabbit or chicken portions or serve the sauce separately in a sauceboat.

Poulet Sauté Chasseur Façon Grand-mère

GRANDMOTHER'S CHICKEN CHASSEUR

Ceps or porcini *(the Italian name), are common around Provence. They have a
deep, rich flavor and are wonderful when eaten soon after picking.
If you can't get fresh ones used dried, soaking them first.*

Ceps are displayed on leaves to keep them fresh.

SERVES 4

3 tablespoons olive oil
4 skinless, boneless
chicken breasts
8 shallots, quartered
2 garlic cloves,
finely chopped
Small bunch of fresh thyme
1 bay leaf
4 large tomatoes, peeled and
roughly chopped

1¼ cups dry
white wine
Salt and freshly ground
black pepper
2 ounces ceps, halved or
quartered, or ½ ounce dried
ceps, soaked in warm water
for 20 minutes
2 tablespoons chopped
fresh parsley

1 Heat 2 tablespoons of the oil in a large casserole dish
and sauté the chicken pieces for 5–6 minutes, turning
them occasionally. Remove to a plate.

2 Add the remaining tablespoon of oil and the shallots
and garlic to the pan and sauté for 3–4 minutes, without
browning. Tie the bunch of thyme and bay leaf together.
Return the chicken to the pan with the tomatoes, wine,
herbs and seasoning, and leave to simmer, with the lid on,
for 20 minutes.

3 After 20 minutes add the ceps and cook, uncovered,
for a further 3–4 minutes. Increase the heat and boil
rapidly, to reduce the sauce slightly.

4 Remove the thyme and bay leaf, check the seasoning
and serve, sprinkled with chopped parsley.

Filets de Boeuf au Beurre d'Anchois

FILLET OF BEEF WITH ANCHOVY BUTTER

*This is a very simple dish to prepare and the anchovy butter can
be made in advance. As soon as the steaks are cooked, top them with the slices of
anchovy butter to allow it to melt slightly before being served.*

SERVES 4

4 fillet steaks

FOR THE ANCHOVY BUTTER
4 tablespoons butter,
softened

4 anchovies, mashed
2 garlic cloves,
finely chopped

1 Mix the butter with the anchovies and garlic. Lay a piece of plastic wrap on the work surface and place the butter mixture on it. Lift up one edge of the plastic wrap and lay it over the butter and then roll gently to form the butter into a log about 4 inches long. Wrap in the plastic wrap and refrigerate for 30 minutes to 1 hour, until the butter is hard.

2 Unwrap the butter and cut it into eight equal slices.

3 Cook the steaks to your liking: 2½ minutes on each side for rare, 4 minutes a side for medium, or 6 minutes per side for well done. Place two pieces of butter on top of each steak and serve. The butter will melt gradually during the meal.

Paqueton de Biou au Sauce Tomate

STUFFED BEEF WITH A TOMATO SAUCE

This dish is sometimes called Petits oiseaux sans têtes *which
translates as "small birds with no heads." This refers to the finished dish,
which might be thought to resemble such a thing! Serve with polenta.*

SERVES 4

4 thin rump steaks
3 tablespoons chopped
fresh parsley
8 garlic cloves, crushed
Freshly ground black pepper
4 slices of smoky bacon
3 tablespoons olive oil

FOR THE TOMATO SAUCE
1 tablespoon olive oil

1 small onion,
roughly chopped
14 ounce can of chopped
tomatoes
Small bunch of fresh
thyme, finely chopped
1 bay leaf
⅔ cup white wine
Salt and freshly ground
black pepper

1 The steaks in this dish need to be really thin, so flatten them out with a rolling pin. Place a piece of wax paper over a steak and then roll hard over the steak. Or pound the meat with the rolling pin.

2 Combine the chopped parsley and garlic in a small bowl and season with pepper. Lay a piece of bacon on each steak and top it with a quarter of the parsley and garlic. Roll the steaks up quite tightly and tie them with string at each end.

3 Make the tomato sauce. Heat the oil in a small saucepan and sauté the onion. Add the remaining ingredients and leave to simmer, uncovered, for 5–10 minutes.

4 Heat the oil in a large casserole dish and sauté the steak rolls for 10 minutes, browning them on all sides.

5 Pour the tomato sauce over the beef rolls, cover them with a lid, and cook for a further 30–35 minutes, depending on how well done you like your steak.

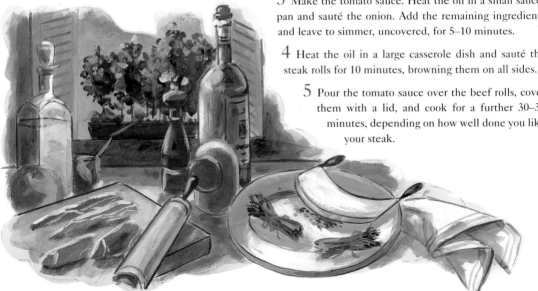

Canard farci à la Mode de Provence

STUFFED DUCK IN THE PROVENÇAL STYLE

*The stuffing in this dish can be used to stuff either a whole duck
or individual duck breasts. Served with baby potatoes and a green
vegetable, this dish makes a simple dinner party idea.*

SERVES 4

1 duck, weighing about
3 pounds or 4
medium-size duck breasts

FOR THE STUFFING
1 tablespoon olive oil
4 shallots, finely chopped
2 garlic cloves, finely
chopped (optional)
4 slices of bacon, chopped
3 ounces brown button
mushrooms, roughly chopped

2 ounces cooked
ham, chopped
2 cups fresh bread crumbs
4 anchovies, roughly chopped
2 eggs, beaten
Handful of fresh sage leaves,
roughly chopped
Liver from the duck, roughly
chopped (optional)
Salt and freshly ground
black pepper

1 Preheat the oven to 375°F. Heat the olive oil in a saucepan and gently sauté the shallots and garlic for 3–4 minutes. Add the bacon and sauté for a further 2–3 minutes. Remove from the heat and add the remaining stuffing ingredients, mixing well.

2 If using a whole duck, remove any excess fat. Place the stuffing in the cavity and season the duck with salt and pepper. Score the skin several times with a knife. Stand the duck on a rack in a roasting pan and roast in the oven for 1½ hours. Every 30 minutes, remove the duck from the oven and carefully pour off the fat.

3 Carve the duck at the table, serving each diner with the stuffing as well.

4 If using duck breasts, pierce the skin several times or score the skin a few times to release some of the fat. Carefully make a pocket in each breast by slicing horizontally through, leaving ¼ inch uncut at both edges and at the back. Alternatively if using breasts with

A garlic seller.

skins on, partially peel the skin from the meat, insert the stuffing, and pull the skin back into place. Put the breasts on a rack in a roasting pan and cook in a medium oven for 50 minutes to 1 hour.

S ubtle is not the word that comes to mind when singing the praises of Provençal cuisine. Unlike the more sophisticated cooking of Paris, Burgundy, Normandy and the Loire, that of the sunny south has never been reticent in its use of herb and spice. Nowhere is this more apparent than in the sauces, purées and dips native to its table.

Garlic rules with an arrogance born of its fabled place in the Provençal kitchen, lending its bold accents to many basic preparations that are then used in other dishes. It is fair to say that any dish styled à la Provençale in a cookery book or on a menu will breath its pungent fumes. Garlic even asserts its power over that unctuous cosmopolitan, mayonnaise, transforming it into aïoli at the crush of mortar against pestle (or, less prosaically, in the now ubiquitous food processor).

Sauces, Dips and Pastes

BASIL PASTES

Nice is the home of *pistou*, a kind of basil paste, named for the small-leaved basil found only in these warmer climes. While it bears an unmistakeable resemblance to the better-known *pesto* of Genoa, it replaces the Parmesan cheese

with Gruyère (Nice), Gruyère and Parmesan mixed (Marseilles), or even Gorgonzola (in the coast around Hyères). Traditionally, the paste did not contain pine nuts; they have now crept in, a result of the unbeatable popularity of the Italian version.

While the garlicky, red peppery *rouille* is used only as a complement to fish soups, *aïoli* has gained a far wider culinary acceptance, finding its way not only into *bourride* and sometimes *soupe aux poissons*, but also serving as a dip for uncooked vegetables – carrots, radishes, celery and the like – as well as more traditionally, featuring in *le grand aïoli*, alongside a huge platter of boiled cod and (in Marseilles and Nîmes) snails,

Chief among the characteristic flavors of the region is that of garlic – without which no sauce Provençale deserves the name.

and cooked vegetables – carrots, green beans, potatoes – together with a salad of tomatoes and onions.

"The Poor Man's Caviar"

Garlic finds its way into two other typical dips or spreads, *tapénade* and *anchoïade*. Sometimes called "the poor man's caviar" (also the *soubriquet* for a herby eggplant purée found less frequently), *tapenade* is the purple-black of its main constituent, the oily, pitted black olives of Marseilles. Its name, however, derives from the Provençal word for another ingredient – *tapéno* (capers) – an essential which is nevertheless omitted in less authentic recipes. In addition to its more common use, spread on toast or bread, it is also delicious mixed with the yolk of hard-boiled egg and restuffed into the white.

In *anchoïade*, the prime ingredient is salted anchovy fillets, pounded to a paste with garlic, olive oil, vinegar and thyme or *herbes de Provence*. Though encountered all over

the south, it was the gift of Avignon, a town whose position inland and chosen seat of the fourteenth-century papacy made it an early and enthusiastic consumer of preserved fish. A more basic anchovy paste is a combination of salted fillets and herbs – in the old days, left to marinate for a month – known as *pissalat*. This gave its name to *pissaladière* and its inimitable flavor to another staple of its inventive home town, *salade Niçoise*.

There are other recipes for local pastes, pâtés and spreads that are far harder to find today. One is *pâté des grives*, made from the flesh of that plump songbird, the thrush. Today it is, happily, illegal to kill them; but in more remote towns and villages, you can still see *pâté des oiseaux* on the menu – make of it what you will.

Poutargue does not suffer from the same ban, but it is even more elusive for the detective-gourmet. A specialty of Martigues, once a village 25 miles outside Marseilles but today, because of unchecked ribbon development, virtually a suburb, it is the dried roe of the female grey mullet (*muge*), which bred in the waters of the Étang de Beurre. Once the erstwhile village lived by fishing, but today that industry has been supplanted by others. In its old-fashioned form, the roe was salted, flattened and hung to dry; slices were cut off and eaten as appetizers, with the local wine. Today, being the rarity that it is, roe is much more expensive – and it is usually extended by being mashed with olive oil and herbs, resulting in a taste similar to taramasalata. Mauritania is a new source of cheaper roes, much as Hungary has become for a percentage of France's nominal *foie gras*.

But it is probably sauce Provençal that becomes the most familiar sight on any menu in the south of France; it can mean many things, depending upon the meat, fish, fowl or vegetable it appears with. However, when hot, it will most likely contain – in addition to garlic – onions and tomatoes sweated in olive oil, with stock and wine stirred in. Cold, it classically combines olive oil, vinegar, seasoning, garlic, peeled and crushed tomatoes, gherkins, and parsley. There is no better complement to a fresh fish, or to a beef or lamb salad, than this tangy accompaniment, redolent of a warm, earthy region.

France's greatest port, Marseilles has played host to centuries of invaders and immigrants. The garlicky, peppery rouille that accents its famous bouillabaisse is a close relation to the harissa of the Maghreb Arab.

Anchoïade

ANCHOVY SAUCE

*This is a paste that can be used as a dip for crudités or as a spread
for triangles of toast. You can make a more substantial snack by following
the additional steps at the end of the recipe.*

MAKES 1½ CUPS

2 garlic cloves, finely
chopped
5 ounces anchovy fillets in
oil, drained
1 tablespoon white-wine
vinegar

1 cup olive oil
1 tablespoon finely chopped
fresh parsley
Freshly ground black pepper

1 Place the garlic in a bowl and add the anchovy fillets. Crush the garlic and anchovies together with the back of a wooden spoon.

2 Add the vinegar and a tablespoon of oil and mash them into the paste. Continue adding the olive oil slowly, mixing well after each addition.

3 Add the parsley and a few turns of black pepper.

4 To make a substantial snack, soak several triangles of bread in olive oil and spread the *anchoïade* on one side of the bread. In a separate bowl, make up a mixture of fresh bread crumbs, chopped fresh parsley and chopped garlic, and sprinkle each triangle with the mixture.

5 Place the bread triangles on a baking sheet and bake in the oven 375°F for 8–10 minutes.

Cook's Tip

One of the best ways of serving anchoïade
and many of the dips in this chapter is with crudités.
You can be as creative as you wish with a platter of
crudités; use some of the more unusual vegetables, such
as baby artichoke hearts, asparagus tips and Belgian
endive. Place the dips in ramekins on a large platter
and surround them with raw vegetables.

The French use day-old bread for toasts and croûtons.

Sauce Tomate

TOMATO SAUCE

*So many Provençal recipes make use of a tomato sauce. Scattered
throughout the book are several different ways of making tomato sauce; the
one below is a good one for serving with meats and on pasta.*

SERVES 4

1 tablespoon olive oil
2 garlic cloves,
finely chopped
1 onion, finely chopped
1 carrot, sliced
2 celery stalks, finely sliced
1½ pounds fresh tomatoes,
peeled and chopped finely, or
2 cans of chopped tomatoes

1 teaspoon sugar
Bunch of fresh thyme
Fresh rosemary sprig
1 bay leaf
Fresh parsley sprig
1 tablespoon fresh
lemon juice
Salt and freshly ground
black pepper

1 Heat the oil in a large saucepan and sauté the garlic, onion, carrot and celery for 5 minutes, until all the vegetables are soft.

2 Add the chopped tomatoes and sugar. Tie the herbs together to make a bouquet garni and add it to the sauce.

3 Simmer for 20 minutes. If you prefer a chunky sauce, simply stir in the lemon juice, season and serve. If you require a smooth sauce, push the sauce through a fine strainer, and then add the lemon juice and seasoning. Return to a clean pan and gently reheat.

Rouille

RED-CHILI MAYONNAISE

Rouille *is traditionally served with* bouillabaisse *and sometimes with other Provençal fish soups, where it tops slices of toasted French bread sprinkled with cheese.* Rouille *means "rust", which is the color of this sauce.*

MAKES 1 GOOD CUP

½ dried or fresh red chili or 2 teaspoons cayenne pepper	2 egg yolks
4 garlic cloves	Salt
	½ cup olive oil

1 Remove the seeds from the chili, if using, and cut it into small pieces. Pound the chili or cayenne, garlic, egg yolks and a little salt, using a pestle and mortar, until smooth.

2 Slowly work in the olive oil, drop by drop, until the mixture thickens. Do not add the oil too quickly or the sauce will separate. Alternatively, the sauce can be made in a blender, adding the oil slowly while the blender is running. If the oil is added too quickly, it will curdle.

Tapenade

OLIVE AND ANCHOVY PURÉE

Tapenade *can be used in a variety of ways. Try spreading it on small triangles of toast and serving as a canapé; for a more substantial snack, mix with hard-boiled yolk as a stuffing for eggs.*

MAKES JUST UNDER 1 CUP

8 ounces black olives, pitted	2 tablespoons capers, drained and rinsed
2 garlic cloves	1 tablespoon lemon juice
2-ounce can of anchovy fillets, drained	4 tablespoons olive oil

1 Mash together all the ingredients, except the olive oil, using a mortar and pestle – or a blender – until you have a purée. Then add the olive oil gradually (with the blender running).

2 If a thinner consistency is required, simply add more olive oil.

Purée d'Aubergine Au Chèvre

EGGPLANT DIP WITH GOAT'S CHEESE

Serve this creamy purée as a spread for toast or as a dip for crudités.
This purée can be made in advance and taken on a picnic. Simply stir it before
serving. Baking the eggplant gives it a wonderful smoky flavor.

MAKES 1½ CUPS

1 large eggplant, weighing
about 1 pound
1½ ounces soft goat's cheese
1 garlic clove, finely chopped
5 fresh basil leaves

1 tablespoon roughly
chopped fresh dill
1 tablespoon roughly
chopped fresh oregano
1 tablespoon lemon juice

1 Preheat the oven to 375°F. Prick the eggplant all over and bake it in the oven for 40 minutes, until soft.

2 Leave the eggplant to cool slightly and then cut it in thick slices, without peeling it.

3 Place the eggplant in a food processor and blend it for 30 seconds. Add the remaining ingredients and blend until smooth.

The wooden "cages" hold maturing goat's cheese.

Pistou

BASIL SAUCE

The most famous use of pistou *is as an ingredient in the soup
bearing its name,* soupe au pistou *(page 26).* Pistou *can also be mixed
into fresh pasta or eaten with fish and shellfish.*

MAKES ABOUT ⅓ CUP

2 garlic cloves, quartered	2 ounces Parmesan cheese,
5 fresh basil leaves	cut in matchsticks
	2–3 tablespoons olive oil

1 Using a mortar and pestle pound the garlic cloves into a paste. Tear up the basil leaves and add a few at a time, pounding until you have a dark green paste. Add the cheese matchsticks, a few at a time, and continue to pound until you have a creamy texture. Gradually add the olive oil until the mixture resembles creamy mayonnaise.

2 It is preferable to make the *pistou* using a pestle and mortar to achieve the authentic texture. However, if this is not possible, add the garlic, basil and cheese to a blender and purée them. Gradually drizzle in the oil until the mixture thickens.

Aïoli

GARLIC MAYONNAISE

*This is a garlic mayonnaise that can be eaten with raw and cooked vegetables or
added to soups, both as a thickener and for flavor. It is often found accompanying*
la bourride *(see page 50) and is the centerpiece of* le grand aïoli *(page 19).*

MAKES 1 GOOD CUP

4 garlic cloves, quartered	1 cup olive oil
Salt	Juice of 1 lemon
2 egg yolks	

1 Using a mortar and pestle, crush the garlic with a little salt. Add the egg yolks and pound with the garlic.

2 Add a few drops of olive oil and blend them into the mixture. Continue adding the olive oil very slowly, increasing the amount as the sauce thickens. Once all the oil is incorporated, stir in the lemon juice.

3 If you prefer to use a blender, purée the garlic and egg yolks together first. Then add a few drops of olive oil and blend. Continue adding the oil, drop by drop, and then in a slow, steady stream until the sauce thickens. Add the lemon juice and salt.

Pissalat

MARINATED SARDINE AND ANCHOVY PURÉE

Pissalat is the traditional base of pissaladière *(see page 25), but it is more often made only with anchovies. If you can't find fresh anchovies, use double the amount of sardines. It is also good spread on croûtons.*

MAKES 1½ CUPS

12 ounces small
fresh sardines
12 ounces fresh anchovies
1 ounce coarse salt
Fresh thyme sprig,
roughly chopped

6 cloves
1 tablespoon mixed black
and white peppercorns
6 bay leaves
7 tablespoons olive oil

1 Remove the heads and backbones from the fish. Take a small earthenware dish and place a layer of fish across the bottom.

2 Sprinkle with some of the salt, thyme, cloves, peppercorns and bay leaves. Add another layer of fish and seasoning. Repeat a third time, ending with a layer of salt. Pour over 3 tablespoons of the olive oil. Store in a cool place for 24 hours to allow the flavors to develop.

3 Stir with a wooden spoon. Leave the mixture for a week, stirring every day. At the end of the week it should resemble a purée.

4 Remove the bay leaves and then purée the mixture in a blender or push it through a fine strainer. Place in a jar with the remaining olive oil. Stored in the refrigerator, it should last for two weeks.

Since the best fruit in France is grown in Provence, it is no wonder that the *finale* of most family meals is still fresh fruit, with perhaps the alternative or addition of dried fruit – dates, figs, raisins or prunes – and nuts in season. Locally-grown peeled sweet almonds, wet November–December walnuts, whose ivory flesh is complemented by their surprisingly milky flavor, and roasted pyramids of winter chestnuts, all do service for the dessert course.

The fruitfulness of the countryside is literal: The Bouches-du-Rhône grows some 20 per cent of French pears, and more come from Fréjus on the Riviera, as do peaches, also a product of Avignon. The region of Solies-Pont is famed for its juicy red cherries and figs, though the little green *figue de Marseilles* is the most prized. White and yellow nectarines and plums grow in all departments; lemons, oranges, tangerines, blood oranges and grapefruit are scattered throughout, acting as ornamental trees even in the most built-up areas of the Côte d'Azur. These citrus fruits make elegant and mouthwatering sorbets in the most exclusive

Desserts

and expensive restaurants on that golden coast.

Pastel-fleshed Cavaillon melons are the unmistakeable sign of summer – so ripe and so cheap at the height of the season that they seem to appear automatically at the start of every meal, whether at home or in a local restaurant. For a change, there might be another popular melon, a rich orange canteloupe or an ogen. Sometimes, filled with strawberries or raspberries macerated in champagne or liqueur, they appear at the end of the meal. The flesh of the muscat melon, puréed and heightened with honey, is baked and served cold with fruit preserves, as part of the Christmas festivities in the region north of Aix-en-Provence.

PASTRY DESSERTS
The peasant lifestyle of previous centuries, and the distance between the villages and the *cabanons* of subsistence farmers, meant that other than the fresh fruit provided by Mother Nature, pastry desserts tended to come from one of two traditions. One was that of the professional *boulanger* and *pâtissier*, who worked with yeast doughs and oil- or butter-rich pastries; and the other that of the home cook, who was restricted to quicker, less costly ingredients.

These luscious soft fruits, offered in the Apt market, could well have ended up in the widely-famous preserves and conserves, or candied and packed in attractive little baskets for the busy tourist and export trade.

It was this home – and, later, street-stall – tradition that gave all the recipes for deep-fried pastries: sugared acacia and zucchini-flower fritters; the *chi-chi* of Marseilles – dough spirals fried in fat and dusted in sugar; the *bausias*, "little lies" of northeast Provence and the *oreillettes*, "little ears" of the south, both flavored with lemon- or orange-flower water and fried in oil, and many other variations.

Of the professional tradition, there is, first and foremost, *fougasse*, the holed, fretwork bread of the region. Usually savory – topped with a scattering of herbs or olives – it also occurs in a sweet guise, lifted with the ubiquitous citrus water augmented with candied peel. *Fougassette* refers, not to smaller loaves, but to round, hard biscuits found in Grasse and Vence (and called *chaudeu* in Nice), also flavored with lemon- or orange-flower water. Other sweet country breads occasionally encountered incorporate almond paste, figs or quinces, rolled in sugar or honey and baked into the dough.

As in the rest of France, a full range of tarts make much of the excellent soft and citrus fruit of the region; *tarte au citron* being typical. More idiosyncratic specialties include *tarte Tropeziénne*, a soft yeast and egg dough, filled with custard cream and covered with crunchy crystalized sugar, and *panade*, a traditional Christmas tart from the Var made with sweetened pumpkin.

FLAVORED HONEY
Before processed sugar became easily available, honey was the customary sweetener, and it is still an important source of income for a large contingent of small producers. Provençal honey is a luxury item, flavored with flowers of lavender, of wild thyme and of other mountain herbs; with jasmine and citrus blossom. Lesser varieties are used to make the *nougat noir* (black nougat) of Sault-en-Vaucluse, Draguigan and St Tropez, colored with caramelized sugar and packed with split almonds. The more well known white

nougat – speckled with pistachios or pine nuts and glacéd fruit – is associated with Montelimar, though also made elsewhere. *Nougat glacé* is a delicious ice cream.

Honey was also once used to coat the preserved fruits of Apt; today, sugar glazes the whole miniature peaches, figs, plums and cherries, the slivers of melon and citrus peel. They are sold – wrapped in characteristic rush baskets or packed into colorful tins, along with luscious jams made from the same fruits – in the shops and market of the town.

But sweetest of the sweets are the litany of confections associated with towns all over the region. There are Aix-en-Provence's *calissons*, eliptical candies of melon paste covered with marzipan icing; records of its manufacture exist from plague times, when it was regarded as a panacea. The *berlingots* of Carpentras – triangular multi-striped humbugs – can trace their lineage to the time of the first Avignon Pope, Clement V. Their name is a corruption of his own – Bertrand de Gotz. Tarascon's chocolate *tartardines* commemorate a Quixote-like character, Tartarin, invented by Provençal native son Alphonse Daudet, in 1872. From the borders of Monaco come *grimaldines*, orange chocolates named for the royal family; from Nîmes, almond crisp *croquants*; *mendiants* from Toulon and *marrons glacés* from Collobrieres. Such packets, tins and boxes of delights could make a charming collection and a wonderful souvenir of a sojourn in Provence.

Everyone's idea of the good life in the south of France – a pavement cafe, tables set and waiting for the midday influx of customers.

Fougasse

FLAT YEAST BREAD

Fougasse is one of the desserts served at Les treize desserts *on Christmas Eve. Fougasse is often the centerpiece, representing Christ on the cross. It can be either sweet, as in this recipe, or savory, depending on the filling.*

MAKES 2 LOAVES

1 pound strong white bread flour	Juice and zest of half an orange
2 teaspoons dried yeast	1 tablespoon honey
½ teaspoon salt	2 teaspoons orange-flower water
1 tablespoon sugar	1 ounce candied peel, cut in small pieces (optional)
1 large egg, beaten	
3 tablespoons olive oil	

1 Combine the flour, yeast, salt and sugar in a large bowl.

2 In a separate bowl or jug, combine the egg with the oil, orange juice, honey and orange-flower water. Add 3–4 tablespoons of hot water or sufficient to make the liquid up to 7½ fluid ounces. Mix well.

3 Make a well in the center of the flour and pour in the wet ingredients. Gradually draw the flour into the center, mixing it with the liquid. Then use your hands to form a dough. If the mixture appears too dry to form into a dough, add more water, a tablespoon at a time.

4 Turn the dough onto a lightly floured work surface and knead for 10–15 minutes, until the dough is smooth.

5 Return the dough to the bowl, cover with a cloth and leave to rise in a warm place for 1 hour, or until doubled in size.

6 Return the dough to a floured work surface and knead for a further 1–2 minutes. Divide the dough in half and roll each one into an oval about ½ inch thick. Make several deep incisions right through the dough and pull the holes apart, to prevent them closing up during cooking. Stud the dough with the small pieces of candied peel, if using.

7 Place the loaves on a greased baking sheet, cover with a cloth and leave to rise for a further 45 minutes to 1 hour. Preheat the oven to 400°F.

8 Bake in the oven for 20–25 minutes. To test if they are cooked, lightly tap the bottom of the loaves; if they sound hollow, they are ready. Leave to cool before eating.

Melon de Cavaillon aux Framboise

CAVAILLON MELON WITH RASPBERRIES

*Cavaillon is the great melon center of Provence. In the height of summer,
deliciously sweet honeydew and cantaloupe melons can be seen piled high in the
markets. Here the melon is mixed with another great summer flavor, the raspberry.*

SERVES 4

4 small Cavaillon, Cantaloupe or Charentais melons	1 pound raspberries
	8 tablespoons port
	4 teaspoons sugar

1 Cut a slice off the top of each melon, reserving it for later. Remove any seeds. Carefully scoop out the flesh with a melon baller or with a spoon, and place it in a bowl.

2 Add the raspberries to the bowl, pour over the port and sprinkle over the sugar. Mix well.

3 Divide the fruit mixture between the emptied-out melons and replace the lids.

4 Place the melons on a large serving platter and surround with cracked ice. Leave for several hours in a cool place (not the refrigerator) to chill. It is not advisable to place cut melon in the refrigerator, since its strong aroma can transfer to other food.

Cook's Notes

As a dramatic end to a summer meal, place all the prepared melons on a large serving platter and then surround them with crushed ice and additional raspberries and scatter mint leaves around.

Melons and soft fruit are natural allies.

83

Figues Pochées aux Vin Blanc et Miel

FIGS POACHED IN WHITE WINE AND HONEY

*Fig trees, like olive trees, are a common sight all over Provence.
When there is a profusion of figs, the people of Provence gather them for
drying and making into jams and liqueurs.*

The abbey of Senanque is renowned for its lavender oil.

SERVES 4

1¼ cup sweet, fruity white wine	Grated zest and juice of 1 lemon or lime
2 tablespoons flavored or ordinary honey	Pinch of grated nutmeg
	8 figs

1 Combine all the ingredients, except the figs, in a saucepan and bring to a boil. Add the figs whole and poach for 2–3 minutes.

2 Remove the figs to a serving dish. Increase the heat under the sauce and reduce it by half.

3 Pour the sauce over the figs and allow it to cool. Keep refrigerated until ready to serve. Serve with cream, ice cream or sour cream.

Cook's Notes

If you can't get fresh figs, try using peaches, apricots or nectarines instead. Simply halve and stone the fruit before placing it in the poaching liquid. It is important to use a sweet wine for this dish or the sauce will be quite bitter.

Oreillettes

LITTLE EARS

These little pastry biscuits were traditionally a New-Year treat,
but are now available all year round. They are called "little ears," because
they resemble ears when they are cooked!

MAKES ABOUT 70 BISCUITS

3 tablespoons butter	1 tablespoon orange-flower water
1⅔ cups all-purpose flour	flower water
Pinch of salt	Grated zest of 1 orange
½ teaspoon baking powder	About 5 cups sunflower oil,
2 eggs, beaten	for deep-frying
	Confectioner's sugar

1 Melt the butter in a small saucepan over a very gentle heat. As soon as it melts, remove from the heat and leave to cool until ready to use.

2 Sift the flour, salt and baking powder into a bowl. Make a well in the center and pour in the eggs, orange-flower water, melted butter and orange zest.

3 Gradually draw the flour into the center, incorporating the wet ingredients into the flour. Mix to form a dough, with all the ingredients thoroughly blended.

4 Form the dough into a ball, place it in a plastic bag and chill for 2 hours.

5 Roll the dough out to ⅛–¼ inch thick. The thinner the dough is rolled, the crunchier the *oreillettes* will be. Using a pastry cutter or a knife, cut the dough into 2-inch squares. Then cut each square in half to form a triangle.

6 Cut a slit along the base of each triangle and pull the tip of the triangle through the slit, to resemble an ear.

7 Heat the oil in a deep-fat fryer or large saucepan to 375°F, or until a cube of bread dropped in floats to the surface and turns golden within about 30 seconds. Fry the *oreillettes* a few at a time for a few seconds, until golden. Drain on paper towels, allow to cool and then sprinkle with confectioner's sugar. The *oreillettes* will puff up as they cook.

Millassette "Lily"
GREAT-AUNT LILY'S CAKE

This is a recipe belonging to a friend's great-aunt Lily, who lives in Provence.
It is a recipe she has been using all her life and was given to her by her mother.
Millassette *is a cross between a flat cake and a pancake.*

SERVES 4–6

1 cup milk	4 eggs, separated
½ cup caster sugar	½ cup all-purpose flour
½ vanilla pod	

1 Preheat the oven to 400°F. Place the milk in a saucepan, with the sugar and vanilla pod. Bring to a boil. Remove from the heat and leave to infuse for 10 minutes. Then remove the vanilla pod.

2 Stir in the egg yolks and flour and use a whisk to combine the ingredients thoroughly.

3 In a separate bowl, beat the egg whites until stiff.

4 Add a tablespoon of the milk mixture to the egg whites, to slacken them. Continue adding the mixture a few tablespoons at a time, folding the mixture together carefully so you don't knock out too much air.

5 Grease a shallow baking pan (approximately 12 x 19 inches), or a pan with a similar surface area. Pour the batter into the greased pan and bake in the oven for 45 minutes. Allow to cool before cutting into wedges. Serve it as great-aunt Lily does, with fresh figs and peaches.

Tarte aux Noix et Miel

WALNUT AND HONEY TART

The sight of lavender fields in Provence is spectacular. The lavender is often used to flavor honey and if you can find lavender-flavored honey, it would make this tart even more Provençal and delicious.

SERVES 6

FOR THE SWEET PASTRY	FOR THE FILLING
1 cup all-purpose flour	2 eggs
½ teaspoon salt	2 ounces sugar
4 egg yolks	1 tablespoon all-purpose flour
6 tablespoons superfine sugar	2 tablespoons flavored honey,
¾ cup ground almonds	such as lavender or heather
1 stick (4 ounces) unsalted	3 ounces walnut pieces
butter, softened	4 tablespoons butter, melted

1 To make the pastry, sift the flour and salt into a large bowl. Make a well in the center and add the egg yolks, sugar, ground almonds and butter. Using your fingertips only, work together the ingredients in the well, and then gradually draw in the flour to form a soft dough. Place the dough in a plastic bag and chill for 30 minutes.

2 Preheat the oven to 375°F. To make the filling, beat the eggs and sugar together until light and fluffy. Then add the flour, honey, walnut pieces and melted butter and mix well.

3 Roll out the dough on a lightly floured work surface to line a 10–11-inch tart pan.

4 Tip the mixture into the pastry case and spread it over the base, smoothing the top.

5 Bake in the oven for 45 minutes. Check the tart 10 minutes before the end of the cooking time and if it appears to brown too quickly, reduce the heat to 350°F. Serve warm or at room temperature. It goes well with honey or vanilla ice cream.

Almond blossom is a familiar sight in early spring.

Nougat Glacé au Coulis de Framboise

NOUGAT ICE CREAM WITH A RASPBERRY COULIS

*All around Provence, this ice cream is served in the restaurants and cafés. It is
best to make it the day before, to insure it will be frozen. The raspberry coulis makes
a refreshing accompaniment, although the ice cream can also be served on its own.*

SERVES 4–6

2 ounces crystalized or glacé
fruit, such as oranges,
pineapples, lemons
and cherries
3 tablespoons rum
2 egg whites
½ cup superfine sugar
⅔ cup heavy cream, lightly
whipped

FOR THE PRALINE
¾ cup blanched almonds
½ cup superfine sugar

FOR THE RASPBERRY COULIS
8 ounces raspberries
3 tablespoons superfine sugar

1 Preheat the oven to 457°F. Place the crystalized fruit in
a bowl, pour over the rum and leave it to macerate for 2–3
hours.

2 To make the praline, place the almonds on a baking
sheet and toast them in the oven for 3–4 minutes. Place
the superfine sugar in a small saucepan over a high heat
and stir constantly with a wooden spoon until the sugar
melts and turns the color of caramel. Add the toasted
almonds, mix well, and remove from the heat.

3 Pour the almonds and sugar out onto a greased marble
slab or baking sheet, spread them out and let them set
and go brittle. Once hard, break into small pieces, either
by using a knife carefully to cut the praline into small
slivers, or by placing the praline in a plastic bag, sealing
the bag and hitting it with a rolling pin several times until
the pieces are the required size.

4 Place the egg whites in a clean, dry bowl and beat
them until very stiff.

5 Place the superfine sugar in a small saucepan, add 2
tablespoons water and mix well. Melt the sugar over
medium-high heat. Stir constantly, boiling until the sugar
reaches 250°F on a sugar thermometer. If you do not have
a sugar thermometer, drip a small drop of the sugar
mixture into a bowl of cold water. If it forms a small, soft
ball, the sugar is ready.

6 Once the sugar is hot enough, pour it into the beaten
egg whites and beat immediately. Beat for 3–4 minutes,
until the mixture is smooth and shiny and looks similar to
meringue.

7 Drain the crystalized fruit. Fold the cream, crystalized
fruit and praline into the egg-white mixture and mix well.

6 Line a 1 pound loaf pan or individual ramekins with
plastic wrap and pour in the mixture. Freeze for at least 4
hours, or until the mixture is of ice cream consistency.

7 To make the raspberry coulis, purée the fruit in a
blender until smooth, and then push it through a strainer
to remove the seeds. Stir in the sugar.

8 To serve, turn out of the individual ramekins or cut the
ice cream loaf into individual slices. Serve two slices per
person, arranging the slices at an angle to each other.
Serve surrounded by the raspberry coulis.

Tarte au Citron

LEMON TART

Although the majority of the French lemon crop comes from Corsica, many families obtain their lemons from trees in their gardens. This dish has a surprise for each guest: slices of caramelized lemon at the bottom of the tart.

SERVES 4–6

FOR THE SWEET PASTRY
¾ cup all-purpose flour
Large pinch of salt
2 egg yolks
3 tablespoons superfine sugar
Few drops of vanilla extract
4 tablespoons unsalted
butter, softened

FOR THE FILLING
3 lemons
⅔ cup superfine sugar
2 eggs
1 stick (4 ounces) unsalted
butter, melted

1 To make the pastry, sift the flour and salt into a large bowl. Make a well in the center and add the egg yolks, sugar, vanilla extract and butter. Using your fingertips only, work the ingredients together in the well. Then gradually draw in the flour, to form a soft dough. Place the dough in a plastic bag and chill it for 30 minutes. Preheat the oven to 375°F.

2 Meanwhile, take one of the lemons and slice it thinly, discarding any pips and both end-slices. Place 2 ounces of the superfine sugar in a large saucepan with 3 tablespoons water and heat until the sugar dissolves. Add the lemon slices and stir, insuring all the slices are coated with the sugar solution. Reduce the heat to very low and gently caramelize the lemon slices for 40–50 minutes. If the saucepan should dry out, add a little more water and reduce the heat even lower, if possible.

3 Roll out the dough on a lightly floured work surface, to line a 10–11 inch tart pan. Grease the pan and line it with the pastry. Line the pastry with foil, weigh it down with baking beans or dried beans, and bake blind for 12–15 minutes. Remove from the oven, discard the foil and beans, and leave to cool slightly. Place a baking sheet in the oven to heat.

4 Now make the filling. Grate the zest of the remaining 2 lemons and squeeze the juice from 1 lemon and half of the other. Cream together the eggs and remaining sugar, until creamy. Stir in the lemon juice and zest, followed by the melted butter.

5 Arrange the caramelized lemon slices in the base of the tart and pour the filling over. Put the tart on the hot baking sheet and bake for 25–30 minutes, until the filling is golden brown and set. Allow to cool slightly before serving with ice cream, cream or yogurt.

Menu Planner

Vegetables play an important role in Provençal cooking, but are rarely just a side dish. They are incorporated into omelets and pastas and lend their vigorous accents to sauces. First courses exploit fresh produce in crudités and soups, as well as in whole vegetables presented either stuffed or marinated in a vinaigrette dressing. Fish is often grilled or served cold as a first course. Country people take their main meal at midday, the men having enjoyed a casse-croûte of bread, pâté, sausage and cheese between breakfast and lunch.

ALFRESCO LUNCH FOR 6

Ravioli à la Niçoise 32
ravioli with meat and spinach

Salade Niçoise 24

Crevettes au pastis 46
shrimps flambéed in pastis

Moules farcis à la Mireille 42
stuffed mussels

Melon de Cavaillon au framboise 83
Cavaillon melon with raspberries

Or

Nougat glacé 88
nougat ice cream

FISHERMAN'S LUNCH FOR 6

Bouillabaisse 51
mixed fish soup (and plenty of bread)

Boiled potatoes

Tarte aux noix et miele 87
walnut and honey tart

SUMMER PICNIC FOR 6

Pan bagnat 18
soaked bread with tuna and salad

Omelette aux artichauts 33
artichoke omelet
Pissaladière 25
onion tart with olives and anchovies

Raw vegetables with
Aïoli 76, *Tapenade* 74 and *Purée d'aubergine* 75

Salade Niçoise 24

Tarte au citron 89
lemon tart

LIGHT LUNCH FOR 4

Gnocchi with tomato sauce 30, 73

Rougets de roche engrillés à la valérie 44
red mullet with Provençal herbs

Salade Mesclun 35
mixed leaf salad

Figues pochées aux vin blanc et miel 84
figs poached in white wine
and honey

FISH SUPPER WITH FRIENDS FOR 4

Moules à la Provençale 49
mussels with garlic and tomatoes

Thon à la Provençale 47
tuna with Provençal vegetables

Ratatouille 23
Provençal vegetable stew

Milasette "Lily" 86
(with figs and peaches)

FAMILY SUNDAY LUNCH FOR 6

Asperges au gratin 20
gratin of asparagus

Gigot d'agneau rôti d'ail 61
roast lamb with garlic

Tian de courgette et tomates 27
zucchini and tomatoes

Tarte au citron 89
lemon tart

PROVENÇAL FEAST FOR 6

Grand aïoli 19

Omelette de fèves à la samiette 35
lima bean and savory omelet

Salade Mesclun 35
mixed leaf salad

Gardiane d'agneau 59
lamb stew with olives

OR

Lapin à l'ail 63
rabbit with garlic

Artichauts à la barigoule 21
artichokes with mushrooms and bacon

Fougasse 82
flat yeast bread

Tarte au citron 89
lemon tart

WINTER DINNER FOR 4

Soupe au pistou 26
vegetable soup with pistou

Boeuf en daube 60
beef casserole

boiled noodles with Gruyère

Tarte au noix et miel 87
walnut and honey tart

SUNDAY LUNCH WITH
FRIENDS FOR 4

Soupe au pistou 26
bean and zucchini soup

Poulet rôti de chèvre et d'ail 58
roast chicken with goat's cheese and garlic

Asperges au gratin 20
gratin of asparagus

Tarte au citron 89
lemon tart

Index

Credits

Quarto Publishing would like to thank the following for permission to reproduce copyright material:
Edmund Nagele/Ace pp 6 & 84, Michael Freeman p 7, Pictor p 8 , Picturebank p 9, Pictor p 11, AA Photo
Library p 12, La Belle Aurore p 16, Pictor p 17, Duncan Davis/Ace p 18, Sopexa (UK) Ltd p 21, Michael
Freeman p 22, J. Allan Cash p 24, Sopexa (UK) Ltd p 26, Edmund Nagele/Ace p 29, Duncan Davis/Ace p 30,
Michael Freeman p 33, Sopexa (UK) Ltd p 35, Image Bank p 38, La Belle Aurore pp 39 & 40, Michael
Freeman p 41, J. Allan Cash pp 42 & 49, Michael Freeman p 50, J. Allan Cash p 53, Michael Freeman p 59,
Picturebank p 60, Michael Freeman p 64, Bo Cederwall/Ace p 67, Michael Freeman p 70, B. Van Berg/Image
Bank p 71, Sopexa (UK) Ltd p 72 & 75, Bullaty/Lomeo/Image Bank p 80, Peter Adams/Ace p 81, Michael
Freeman p 83, Pascal Perret/Image Bank p 87.
While every effort has been made to acknowledge all copyright holders, we apologize if any omissions have
been made.